LIFE

ABOVE

THE

SIMON AND SCHUSTER
NEW YORK

JUNGLE FLOOR,

ĐONALĐ ^R^. ̦PERRY

10   9   8   7   6   5   4   3   2   1

Library of Congress Cataloging-in-Publication Data

Perry, Donald R.
  Life above the jungle floor.

  Bibliography: p.
  Includes index.
  1. Rain forest ecology—Costa Rica.   I. Title.
QH108.C6P474   1986   574.5'2642'0972867   86-20204
ISBN: 0-671-54454-3

Acknowledgments

A book such as this does not materialize without help from numerous persons. I give deep felt thanks to Sylvia Merschel, who gave unending encouragement, support, and creative energy through the many early years that this book was in preparation. While in the field, I was assisted by numerous visitors and researchers at La Selva: Paul Abravaya, Cathy Andrews, Kamaljit Bawa, Jim Beach, Amos Bien, Robert Borth, Phil De-Vries, Gary Freed, Carlos Gomez, Mike Grayum, Charles Griswald, David Janos, Nalini Nadkarni, Dennis Ojima, Cathy Pringle, Manuel Santana, Robert Sanford, and the staff of Finca La Selva and its numerous workers.

I am indebted to Rebecca Eastman, whose belief in this work helped see the book to completion, and to a number of other people who assisted in various ways: Anne-Marie Bennstrom, Rick Gutierez, John Herman, Lee Kavanau, Lynn Nesbit, Mark Oring, Luis Sanjurjo, Stephen Schmidt, Paul Trachtman, David Vescera, and many graduate students associated with the Organization for Tropical Studies.

Some financial support came through Kamal Bawa, Sigma XI, and a grant from California State University Northridge. Osa Productivous Forestales for several years graciously gave me permission to use their facilities at the Osa Peninsula. Additional assistance came from Ron and Marlene Collins, Sheila Selby, and Robert Petricca.

I am grateful to the Costa Rican government and its friendly people, whose parks and foresight stand as examples of human concern for the natural world, for unselfishly allowing me to study in their country.

Finally, I give special thanks to Roberta Halsey, who, besides participating in fieldwork, applied her exceptional editorial talents over long periods to bring the manuscript to final form.

ACKNOWLEDGMENTS

This book is dedicated to my mother and father, who, in their own ways, helped set my course in natural history. And to Andrew Fields, who, after many successful years conducting canopy research, recently lost his life in a tree-climbing accident.

*Yet another continent of life remains to be discov-
ered, not upon the earth, but one to two hundred
feet above it, extending over thousands of square
miles. . . . There awaits a rich harvest for the naturalist who overcomes the obstacles—gravitation, ants,
thorns, rotten trunks—and mounts to the summits of
the jungle trees.*

—WILLIAM BEEBE, 1917
Tropical Wild Life

Contents

Introduction

It seems long ago now, but when I was a child nature's face ra-diated a simplicity and beauty that touched me deeply. On walks, the pastel hues of light passing through spring flower petals caught my eye with an inexplicable attraction, and butterflies seemed out of an unknown, wondrous world. Tall weeds engulfed me and I imagined with clarity, as children do, the adventures a tiny person would encounter in grass jungles that were populated by ferocious beasts of the spider, insect, and reptilian kinds. I still have that curiosity and lust for adventure and it has taken me to a world of plants and animals few people are aware of and fewer still have seen. It is a place beyond childhood dreams, a fragile world that unfortunately, just like a dream, is fading from the earth.

This is the first chronicle ever written about a world found in the treetops of the earth's wet jungles. Many books have attempted to tell of jungle life, but all previous authors, like the explorers about whom they wrote, were prisoners of the dark, humid, and

13

often depressing forest floor. Wildlife near the ground is interesting, but it represents only a fraction of the flora and fauna living in the whole forest. The largest, and in many ways most important, communities are out of reach in an aerial zone called "the canopy." To explore this part of the jungle, one must be able to walk along high limbs like a monkey or travel through the air like winged animals.

The canopy begins at about thirty feet and continues up, tier upon tier, past the height of a seventeen-story building. Scientists using common methods such as collecting poles and extension ladders have a range of about thirty feet, yet two-thirds of jungle plants and animals live above that height; many of these organisms are seldom or never found near the ground. As much as 80 percent of the food for the entire forest is produced in the canopy and in a real sense it is the forest's "main level." Stories about the ground zone tell us little or nothing about the floating kingdom of life that is crucial to the very existence of tropical rain forests.

The main level presents treacherous obstacles to researchers. Working on these long limbs at dizzying heights is much like crawling along a steel girder of a high rise with a few added complications: limbs can sway or break, and they conceal a variety of poisonous animals such as spiders, wasps, vipers, scorpions, and ants. To make matters worse, the trees themselves are weak and can often be heard crashing to the ground during heavy winds. These are only a few of the reasons why the canopy has yet to be thoroughly explored.

Today, as a handful of biologists investigate the canopy, the magnitude of the last century's scientific neglect is beginning to be felt. One can almost hear an uncomfortable rustling in academic halls as new discoveries bring fascinating pieces of the canopy puzzle into place. The emerging picture clearly shows that the canopy has been a foremost habitat in the evolution of life.

One noteworthy study was done by Terry Erwin, a ground-floor biologist whose sights have been held on the jungle's roof. He works at the Smithsonian Institution, where he devised a means of collecting canopy insects from the ground by using pesticides. Through careful examination of thousands of specimens, he has extrapolated that tropical treetops could hold between ten and thirty million species. This figure is staggering. It is up to twenty times greater than all previous estimates of the number of insect species on the planet. From a different angle, this figure would suggest that easily 50 percent of the earth's species live in the canopy.

Most of these insects are locked into an obscure life cycle and are practically invisible. Some that never directly interact with us nevertheless offer unexpected benefits for human life. For example, a vast spectrum of both juvenile and adult insects are folivorous and have evolved a complex biochemical relationship with plants. Plants of many types, including canopy plants, "slap" these hungry hordes with protective chemicals much the same as we spray crops with pesticides. These chemicals are produced within plant cells, and their concentration can be high enough to kill predators.

Since the canopy is the most botanically diverse ecosystem on the planet, we can expect that it holds an incredible reservoir of undiscovered plant-protective chemicals, all as different as the vast range of canopy plants. Aside from affecting insect predators, these chemicals are also physiologically active in arboreal primates and man. Norman Myers, a tropical ecologist, has estimated that approximately $40 billion worth of drugs containing active chemicals from plants are used worldwide every year. It is a distressing fact that drug companies have not even scratched the surface of exploring a jungle's pharmacological wealth.

The canopy is a mixture of known and unknown biology whose usefulness extends far beyond its commercial value as wood and other products. It is an intricate factory of evolutionary ideas that has transformed the earth's life. The influence of this habitat can be found in the aquatic flight of penguins, in a can of mixed nuts, in the wing of a bat, in a parrot's communication, and in the development of the human mind. If we are ever to fully understand the working of life in jungle treetops, some sophisticated systems of access must be devised.

New knowledge about the world in which we live, be it in the sciences or arts, depends as much upon inventions as it does upon ideas. Consider the telescope, microscope, Aqua-lung, and transistor: these were inventions that gave birth to broad fields of science. But where invention flounders, the pursuit of knowledge is stifled, and just such a situation exists today with regard to the most complex of earth's biological communities.

In our quest for knowledge we often spare no expense. Several million dollars have been spent on a project called SETI—the Search for Extraterrestrial Intelligence. Astronomers are listening to radio emissions from distant stars and galaxies for signals made by intelligent forms of life, even though the possibility of finding these signals is admittedly very remote. Tropical forest research receives about $20 million a year from American institutions, but these funds are funneled primarily into studies that can be accomplished at the jungle floor. Canopy research receives no significant funding, yet it is no less important than SETI or a forest's lowest zone—in fact, the canopy holds the most complex communities of life that have ever existed on this planet.

The tropics, and especially the lowland rain forests of Costa Rica where this photojournalistic adventure takes place, are unfathomably intricate and contain a biological opulence that humbles even the best thinkers. Understanding jungle life is a never-ending process, one that requires ground-loving apes to strive to regain what has been evolutionarily lost—an ability to freely roam, explore, and survive in the tops of jungle trees.

Like any idea or innovation, this biological adventure had a moment that could be called its beginning. Rarely are these moments true beginnings; important events often precede them that can sometimes be the first clues along a path to an important destination. This was the case in the fall of 1973 when I went on a weekend hang-gliding adventure with John Williams, a close friend.

Our Volkswagen labored up a highway in the Santa Monica Mountains of coastal California as we headed for an abandoned fire lookout station overlooking Topanga Canyon. Chinook winds that rose up the steep cliffs and crags would provide fantastic lift and, we hoped, the opportunity to soar for hours.

We walked down the dirt road to the station carrying the fifty-pound load on our shoulders without saying a word. The wind whistled through plants and large sandstone rocks, and a bird shot over the ridge like a projectile, holding its wings close to its body. We both wondered if this was the right day for gliding.

The station's instruments told a story that was no longer read. The nervous system of electrical wires had long since been scavenged for valuable copper; recording devices were also gone. But still functioning were the blades of a wind-driven electric generator that had fused into a transparent gray doughnut, driven to insane speeds by the gusts. The cups of the air-speed indicator were in the same frenzied state. My hand-held air-speed indicator measured gusts up to sixty miles per hour, 50 percent faster than the maximum forward velocity of the hang glider. John decided to fly that day anyway, and I remember that as a very daring decision.

Assembling the glider in the wind was a difficult procedure. When it was finished John stepped to the cliff edge as I helped him control the motion of the craft. His objective would be to nose-dive into the valley where winds would be calmer, fly for an undetermined length of time, and then land on what looked like a postage stamp-sized meadow in the valley far below. Neither of us expected that to be easy.

John took off with a lull in the wind and started to slip down into the valley. Within seconds a new gust arrived and lifted him ten, twenty, then thirty feet above the ridge. I watched him straining to come down; he was caught like a beach ball in a geyser of air. The wind was gradually carrying him backward over the ridge. Adrift in a current he could not fight, he was pulled to the point where winds spilled in huge vortexes and eddies into the ravine below.

Turbulent air could stress the aluminum tubing to its breaking point, and since fighting the wind was useless, John turned to fly with it. Immediately he was washed into the violent currents. The craft looked like a floating potato chip; he was out of control and had drifted into a canyon with no landing site. The sharp-pointed manzanita of the chaparral seemed to stand erect on the far ridge and in the valley, like goose pimples on the back of a stone beast. After several minutes of what John would later calmly refer to as a "frightening ride," the hang glider disappeared from sight and I raced down the hill to see if he had been injured in the landing.

John was safe, but the glider was stuck in the tops of some thirty-foot-tall trees. In order to retrieve it, we would have to dismantle the craft and lower it through a layer of branches. This took an hour and a half during which my initial reluctance for climbing at the ends of precarious branches dissolved and I actually began enjoying myself. My perspective shifted and I had a very distinct impression of being a monkey or an ape.

By itself this experience would have been fairly insignificant, but I was in graduate school at California State University at Northridge and it was time to select an area for field research. I had little idea of what relevant work could be done at the university, a plight perhaps shared by graduate students everywhere, and after looking through the brochures at Career Placement, I came away with a feeling of dull resignation.

I was working in a laboratory as a cellular biologist. These researchers are sometimes known as "cell squashers" because of their sophisticated methods for rupturing cells and sorting through the pieces. I once asked a professor what was in the tube he held, whereupon he replied, "Oh this? Just mitochondria." That was sort of like saying he held the livers of a million cells. The work impressed me, but little did I know of the drudgery that went into playing with cell parts. The project that quickly broke my spirit was a study on the mobility of disassociated sea urchin embryos in an applied electric field and current. I grew pale and listless in "the dungeon," the nickname for the basement cellular biology laboratory.

I escaped to the third floor of the Life Science Building, where George Fissler and Andrew Starrett, both professors and field biologists, had their offices. Andrew Starrett, who would be my supervisory professor for my master's degree, was teaching a course on tropical life in which I learned that virtually nothing was known about the communities in the tops of jungle trees. I soon decided to make that my area of study, taking into account both my recent curious experience of retrieving the hang glider and an article in the June 1973 *Scientific American* by William Denison, which hinted at a method that could possibly be refined for tropical work.

When I told Andy about my plans he was at his desk. I remember him clenching his cigar between his teeth with a "you don't know what you are talking about" expression. To his credit he did not discourage me, but my plans must have seemed rather half-baked since I had never been to the tropics and had never seen tall canopy trees. Andy directed me to Costa Rica where he had done a considerable amount of research. After weeks of preparation, I made my first trip to the jungles of Central America.

A Jungle
Cashew Nut Tree

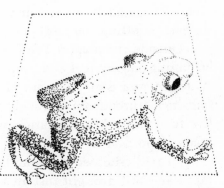

A DRONING, two-cylinder diesel propelled our ferry sluggishly across the bay toward Osa Peninsula, which arose from the mirrored surface of Golfo Dulce like mounds of green velvet. My companion was Rafael Campos, an expert ornithologist from the University of Costa Rica. Rafa had joined me on a quick trip to the wild outlands of his country.

Jungle trees crowded the shore, their leaves shimmering like emeralds in the bright morning light. Golfito, a banana port of the United Fruit Company, was slipping behind. A row of squalid apartments and dormitories, known as pensions, seemed to gaze at us forlornly as we escaped into the immense beauty of this inlet of the Pacific.

I was returning to the Osa anxious to see if the first jungle tree I had ever climbed still stood. It was October of 1982. Four years had elapsed since I had last seen the tree. That was a long time in Costa Rica; a whole new crop of children had arrived, and in order to feed them, more forest had to be cleared for fields of corn and beans.

The sights brought back vivid memories of my first trip to Osa, eight years before in 1974. At that time I was traveling alone with a grand goal—to explore and study the mysteries of natural history hidden high in the forest's roof.

My 1974 flight from Los Angeles was uneventful except for the last half hour. It was late June, Costa Rica's rainy season, and the sky was socked in with billowy cumulonimbus clouds. Humidity, moderately high daytime temperatures—the average monthly temperature is close to 80 degrees Fahrenheit—plus drenching tropical rainstorms charged the isthmus connecting North and South America with floral exuberance. It also made the flight resemble an amusement-park ride. Three passengers were forced to use paper "convenience" bags as the pilot maneuvered around expansive clouds on a stomach-knotting course of descent in order to avoid turbulence.

Outside the airport I felt like one of the dispossessed, with my belongings at my feet and no place to go; I had not yet made living arrangements. I also felt out of place as eyes stared at my six-foot-four-inch frame from a crowd whose average height did not exceed five foot three. My alienation was completed by being a monolingual gringo.

"Taxi," shouted a man, beckoning me toward his cab. The familiar word brought instant relief. He spoke a little English and was able to decipher my Spanish. I frantically leafed through a book of phrases and attempted my first sentence. "Yoh key-air-oh oonah pen-see-own, por-fuh-voar."

It worked. "You want a pension," he replied with a thick Spanish accent.

My destination was not San Jose or one of its excellent hotels, but San Pedro, a suburb and the home of the University of Costa Rica. I was deposited on the sidewalk ten yards away from a railroad crossing. Across the tracks stood the university. The pension, whose name I have forgotten and which no longer exists, was fifty yards down a walkway that ran parallel to the railroad.

The charge for an inelegant, small room with a single bed, communal bath, and a heavily mildewed atmosphere was two dollars per day, a figure that fit nicely into the budget of an unemployed graduate student. Breakfast was included in the rate: one egg, bread, and a cup of coffee. An especially good bargain considering the superb quality of coffee in Costa Rica.

An advantage to traveling on a slim budget is that one meets many people and quickly makes friends. The pension was a home away from home for five students from other Central American countries. They soon became good friends, especially after each discovered they could beat me, a gringo, at chess.

The few days I spent in the capital were hectic with purchases of last-minute supplies. Among the food items I bought was a two-pound bag of chocolate-covered almonds made with fine Costa Rican chocolate that comes from the seeds of the cacao tree. These were emergency rations to help buoy my spirits and energy once the grind of serious canopy research began.

San Jose's streets have a European flavor. They are narrow and heavily traveled by cars, buses, pedestrians, and street vendors. The vendors sell a variety of products: leather goods, jewelry, fresh fruits and vegetables, and hardware. My favorites were fresh-squeezed orange juice and sweet pineapple slices for one colon, about ten cents. On nearly every corner hawkers were yelling, "Chances, chances!"; tickets to the upcoming state lottery could be purchased from them.

Plants were widely cultivated in the city. They overflowed from balconies of private homes and high-rise apartment houses. Tropical flowers sprouted from retaining walls, rain gutters, storm drains, roofs, power lines, and from every conceivable niche where moisture lingered long enough for a plant to germinate. Most of these were not domestic plants but the jungle's front line in its constant effort to reclaim developed land.

I decided to travel by bus to Golfito and then take a plane to Rincon, a logging town that provided room and board to biologists studying the excellent tropical communities nearby. Golfito was the nearest city, if it could be called that, to the Osa. It was little more than a number of support businesses that had developed around the banana industry. Some people called it "the armpit of Costa Rica," and not just because it was under the Osa Peninsula, which extended into the Pacific.

The bus ride to Golfito dragged on for eleven hours, during which time we covered less than two hundred miles. It is wise to know enough Spanish to check schedules before using public transportation. I worried for the last six hours that we would arrive in Golfito too late to find lodging. *"No problema,"* said the bus driver.

It was an expression I heard frequently and usually meant there was cause for concern.

The bus stopped in front of a pension on the outskirts of town. As I disembarked I heard undisguised snickering from my fellow passengers and outright laughter as the bus pulled away. My trust in the driver waned as I examined the run-down accommodations he had selected.

It did not take a command of Spanish to recognize the nature of this establishment as three ladies converged on me in the vestibule. They urged me along, pulling on my backpack and arms, each bickering over her claim to the potentially valuable piece of jetsom that had landed on their shore. I managed to pull free, much to their chagrin, and staggered with my load back onto the street to search the row of pensions for one that was not a brothel.

A skinny, bent-over man lead me to a second-floor room in a nearby building. The man was very dirty, he coughed incessantly, and each step up the stairs was an obvious effort. Decades of filth stained the hall.

The room was small and I sat on the bed, which was inches too short, to test the comfort of its straw mattress. I noticed that the walls did not meet the ceiling; the last couple of feet were screened to allow a healthy flow of air. The construction style was dictated by the constraints of tropical heat and humidity. That night I wished the walls had reached the ceiling as it would have saved me from various unpleasantries of the hotel. Waves of stench drifted in from the manager's room next door and his coughing continued through the night. In the morning I found several bites undoubtedly due to bed bugs; I promptly caught a taxi to the airport for my connection to Rincon.

The flight started out normally as we lifted off the airstrip, climbed, banked sharply, and headed out over the blue waters of Golfo Dulce. Then we descended down, down until the single-engine bush plane was flying so close to the water's surface that a leaping sailfish could have gotten caught on the landing gear.

With distinct Latin charm, the pilot began showing off by hugging all topographic relief, including clumps of trees and bushes. His acrobatics were not intended for me, but rather for the young and beautiful woman who sat next to him. The exhibition continued over, sometimes through, sections of dense jungle. Giant tree crowns were not far off either wing tip so I was able to distract myself from the reckless ride by examining limbs heavily laden with a wide assortment of vegetation. This was a preview of what was to come. Openings between trees allowed fleeting glimpses of the ground, which was a breathtaking distance below the forest roof.

Rincon's cluster of white buildings next to the bay was a comforting sight, and within minutes we were bouncing along a gravel runway two miles from town. The plane came to a stop near a complex of buildings that housed and fed the loggers. The day had grown warm and humid and I quickly became drenched with sweat while unloading ninety pounds of equipment.

I climbed into a waiting jeep, riddled with rust and holes, that coughed its way along a gravel road to the logging camp's headquarters. Beyond the airstrip the road ducked into perpetual twilight. Huge trees, some over fifteen stories tall, rose like giant columns, their tops sending out arches of wood and leaves to eclipse the sun. The forest roof was unaffected by the road; it was just another trail in the network of animal paths that wove through the exotic flora of the forest floor.

This was the wildest sector of Costa Rica. The area boasted a wealth of wildlife, picturesque beaches, and rain forests impossible to find anywhere along the entire Pacific coastline of the Western Hemisphere.

I met the logging camp's director, Rich, an expatriated American, sitting under a four-bladed ceiling fan in his office. We talked about my plans, which customarily had not been forwarded to him from the business office in San Jose.

"You want to climb these trees?" The idea was preposterous to him. "Have you done it before?"

"Of course," I lied, not wanting to jeopardize the expedition.

"Our trees are dangerous," he cautioned. "They are swarming with all kinds of things like scorpions, snakes, and ants." He tried to convince me to leave, but I had come a long way and was not about to give up. I attempted to appease him by emphasizing that dangerous animals would be kept at safe distances.

"I doubt you can avoid getting close," he growled sarcastically. "Other 'scientists' have come here knowing what they were doing.

One was studying peccaries, which he claimed were misunderstood and not dangerous. We lost a lot of work time carrying him to the hospital in Golfito. His wounds took over a hundred stitches. . . ." Rich was grinning by the end of the story. This was obviously one of his favorites; it fit his image of field biologists as total fools. The fact is that studying wildlife is not always safe, and I partially agreed with him; I did not want his company to lose work time on my account.

"I am more concerned about your safety on the ground," said Rich in a more serious tone. "The bushmasters and fer-de-lances are very deadly. They can be up to ten feet long and they do not have rattles. Some have even chased people. Last year a worker was bitten and his leg swelled to twice its normal size. He died on the boat ride to Golfito, bleeding from his ears and all of his pores."

Rich's stories were designed to scare me and they proved effective. That evening in my cabin at Rincon I was startled by a loud noise from the ceiling. I glanced up and listened attentively but heard only soft, high-pitched chirps. The attic was occupied by a colony of bats and their guano leaked through the ceiling, causing large brown stains. The scrambling came again but from a new location in the far corner. Through a hole in the plywood protruded a leering procyonid face. A coati, an animal closely related to the raccoon and about the same size, watched my every move. I did not like the spying bug eyes or the tiny trunk hanging into the privacy of my quarters. I have always found staring wall trophies to be offensive, and this living variety was no exception.

According to Frank Chapman in his book *My Tropical Air Castle*, coatis are among the most intelligent mammals. He came to this conclusion while at his research station on Barro Colorado Island in the Panama Canal Zone. No matter how he suspended food out of reach, the coatis were always able to retrieve their reward by climbing along the ropes. There was a possibility that this coati might not be friendly so I claimed my territory by hitting the varmint square in the head with a pair of rolled-up socks. He instantly vanished; the battle line had been drawn.

In the morning I was jolted from sleep by heavy knocking. Doyly, the guide whom Rich had persuaded me to hire, had arrived. I opened the door and was greeted by a face from ages past. His features mirrored those of statues and murals of pre-Columbian Indians. Here was a man who could claim direct ancestry from those remarkable civilizations. He proved to have expert knowledge of wildlife, but more important, he was able to advise me on the strength of tropical trees.

We walked back to the forest near the airstrip. It had once been a mecca for Andrew Starrett, my major professor at California State University at Northridge, and other tropical biologists during the late sixties and early seventies, but because of the conflicting interests between loggers and biologists, only a trickle of scientists now visited the area. A building once owned by the Tropical Science Center stood in near ruin. Its screenless windows and wasp-infested dorm were symbolic of the intellectual silence that had fallen over Rincon.

A hundred yards to the west we came to a small stream, the Agua Buena, which was the boundary for an expanse of virtually untouched forest spanning the peninsula's breadth and length. The area contained a richness unsurpassed in any land, but now it is almost destroyed. We saw scarlet macaws and a king vulture, huge iguana lizards, a boa constrictor, uncountable varieties of insects, and morpho butterflies whose reflective wings flashed beacons of radiant blue sunlight.

I reluctantly stepped into the stream behind Doyly. A submerged limb struck my leg and I jolted back, remembering Andy's warning, "Do not go swimming in rivers that flow from Lake Nicaragua." He knew of a biologist who was stuck at a border checkpoint behind a long line of people waiting for customs. Apparently it was a hot day and the man decided to take a refreshing swim in a nearby river. He was killed by freshwater sharks. I was up to my knees in the Agua Buena, hoping that the stream was too shallow for any ferocious, cartilaginous fish.

The water was crystal clear, evidence that there were no farms upstream. Measurements show that very few nutrients wash away in the streams of undisturbed jungles, making them one of the most frugal of ecosystems. As nutrients are released from decomposing organic material, they are quickly reabsorbed by the roots of hundreds of tree and herb species that lock these precious nutrients into an extremely efficient cycle. The cycle is broken by uncontrolled slash-and-burn agriculture or by heavy logging.

The apparent lushness of tropical forest soils attracts pioneering farmers worldwide. Generally speaking, most soils, once they are exposed, are quickly degraded by torrential rain, a common weather phenomenon of the humid tropics, where storms often drop four to five inches in a single burst. This erodes the layer of delicate topsoil, which muddies streams and leaches away nutrients that were once locked in living vegetation. Without heavy fertilization the land becomes useless within about five years. Jungle extravagance, in most cases, is merely a nutrient mirage.

A barrier of dense vegetation stood on the Agua Buena's far shore. We had come to impenetrable jungle, or so I thought. Without slowing his pace, Doyly hacked a hole in the green wall, then sheathed his machete. Several yards of thick brush had given way to relative openness where plants did not obstruct our movement.

This is contrary to the image that jungles are impassable. The reason is that vegetation grows densely only where sunlight is intense, such as near riverbanks and at the forest's upper surface, high above the ground. The forest floor receives only one-hundredth of the available sunlight as it filters through successive layers of leaves. At best this supports a thin but impressive community of plants that struggle for survival or are adapted to dark conditions.

Here and there the path was dotted by searing patches of pure sunlight that had found a chink in the continuous roof. These spots are the richest source of energy for the basement's undernourished plants, but their leaves receive only a few moments of intense light throughout the day.

The forest's grandeur was beyond words. Of all those who have tried to capture the feeling, W. H. Hudson in his book *Green Mansions* was probably the most successful.

> Roof I call it . . . but it was no more roof-like and hindering to the soaring spirit than the higher clouds that float in changing forms and tints. . . . How far above me seemed that leafy cloud land into which I gazed. . . . Here Nature is unapproachable with her green, airy canopy, a sun-impregnated cloud—cloud above cloud—and though the highest may be unreachable by the eye the beams yet filter through, illuming the wide spaces beneath—chamber succeeded by chamber, each with its own special lights and shadows. Far above me, but not nearly so far as it seemed, the tender gloom of one such chamber or space is

traversed now by a golden shaft of light falling through some break in the upper foliage giving a strange glory to everything that it touches.

The grand spaces, stacked tiers, backlit mosaic of leaves, and gentle mists rising through beams of sunlight like smoke from smoldering candles have prompted more than one observer to compare jungles to cathedrals. The appropriateness of this comparison became obvious as I walked beneath the trees; not only was my person diminished in relation to the tremendous mass of living things, but I more fully understood why the roof remained unconquered.

We searched for hours, examining numerous trees for a perfect specimen to test my climbing methods. Some of the large trees would have sufficed, yet none had the variety of organisms that I suspected could be found on some old forest giants. Although their tops were not generally visible, one could recognize similar species by surface texture: whether the bark was smooth, grooved, fluted, spiny, or bumpy. The color of the bark could not be used to identify trees unless it was nicked, as the true color was often altered by coatings of white, yellow, or brown lichens. Many trees were unique, with no others of their type being found on the walk. Osa's forest may have more than three hundred species of trees: giants, medium sizes, and dwarfs. A light-starved dwarf that is six feet tall may be fifty years old, even though its trunk is only an inch or so in diameter.

Doyly stopped dead, and I nearly collided with him. He pointed to the trail where we were about to step. *"Terciopelo!"* he exclaimed in a firm, clear voice. The spot looked empty except for the usual litter of twigs and leaves. Then, as if by magic, the twigs materialized into a sinuous string of whitish X's on a large coiled form resting ten feet in front of us. It was the most feared pit viper, not only in Costa Rica, but all of Latin America—the deadly fer-de-lance. Unlike many other venomous species, it does not retreat from people and it is quick to strike. The camouflage of the fer-de-lance is superb, and even a large, ten-foot specimen can blend invisibly into the earth.

Hundreds of deaths each year are attributed to this snake and its pit viper relatives. Their venom acts as a neural toxin, anticoagulant, and digestive enzyme. In nature the enzyme serves to help digest large prey such as rabbits, which are swallowed whole. In severe bite cases, when a victim lives, there are always significant amounts of tissue damage that will take a long time, if ever, to heal completely. Rumor has it that back-country residents will actually amputate bitten limbs to avoid what is seen as certain death, even though venom is not injected in a large percentage of cases. For rural farmers, waiting for symptoms to show would be a game of Russian roulette. Antivenin is a must in the field.

Pit vipers, which include rattlesnakes and water moccasins, have two nostril-like openings on either side of the head from which they derive their name. These are sophisticated temperature receptors that can respond to a change of two-thousandths of a degree centigrade, which enables them to pinpoint the location of a mouse from two feet away. This is a definite advantage in the extreme blackness of forest-floor nights.

Like all local residents, Doyly quickly dispatched the fer-de-lance with his machete. This habit of killing snakes is widespread. In the United States, snakes are so misunderstood that harmless and beneficial species are routinely killed. The earth has numerous forest reserves and toxic snakes are a fundamental part of their ecology. Since the planet has ample land already sterilized for human convenience, anyone who intends to destroy snakes should not venture into reserves.

Minutes after encountering the snake, we came upon a recently cleared patch of forest known as a "light gap." Gaps are created when a large limb, tree, or several trees fall and crush underlying vegetation. The hole that forms in the forest roof allows light to penetrate down to the forest floor. This flood of energy starts a complex process of forest healing that involves many types of trees, vines, and smaller plants. Some trees lie dormant for decades "waiting" for just such an opportunity, while others need light and heat for their seeds to germinate. The latter are specialists adapted to colonize openings quickly and effectively. They are fierce competitors in a race between species to reach the sunny roof. Many trees, like *Cecropia*, never grow tall enough to reach the roof, but they can grow quickly, which ensures their position in the race and gives their seeds time to find another gap to begin the process again. It is a perpetual cycle that helps to make tropical forests the most species-rich forests on the earth.

Doyly and I moved through the gap knowing that its opulence would attract rodents, such as pacas and agoutis. Both are favored game animals because of their tender meat. These animals are also prime prey for large pit vipers, which should make one wary about entering light gaps. Fortunately poisonous snakes are uncommon in most forests and extraordinary care need not be taken.

At the far end of the gap, twenty yards away, stood a tree with a trunk over ten feet in diameter. To this day I have not found a larger tree in Costa Rica. The gap's vegetation sprawled up the trunk and blurred its profile, giving it an enigmatic aura not unlike that of Mayan ruins being reclaimed by jungle.

Doyly was dumbfounded. *"Este?"* he asked, his forehead wrinkled with concern. Doyly objected to the tree because of the clutter of life on its trunk; any rational woodsman would have avoided the tree. I nodded, pointing to the plants on the trunk and the fallen red and yellow flowers at his feet. One of my scientific objectives was to study the pollination of tall tropical trees. I especially wanted to learn the exact insect pollinators upon which tall trees—trees having striking flowers, tasty foods, and exotic wood—depended for reproduction. Information gathered while forests are still partially intact will be invaluable if in the future mankind ever attempts to reverse the damage he has done to the environment.

Doyly was emphatically certain, however, that the limbs of this species were strong. Its common name was espavel (*Anacardium excelsum*), which is a species closely related to the cashew nut tree of commerce, as is shown by the scientific name of the commercial tree: *Anacardium occidentale*. Espavel nuts can be eaten or used as fish bait, and if a means of harvesting the nuts could be designed, it could possibly become a commercial crop.

We cleared a small temporary camp and erected a lean-to of ten-millimeter-thick plastic. I set my things under the shelter and in the process frightened a black frog with neon green stripes from under the leaf litter. It was a small poison-dart frog (*Dendrobates auratus*). The common name comes from a practice of the Choco Indians of western Colombia who use alkaloid-based poisons from the skin glands of these frogs on the tips of their blowgun darts. The most toxic dendrobatids are frogs of the genus *Phyllobates*, which produce some of the most potent natural toxins known. The poison is extracted by gently roasting the frogs, then collecting their sweat.

Curiously, dendrobatids are harmless and can be handled, as they have no means of breaking the skin. To have an effect, the toxin must enter scratches or open wounds. One must wonder how the deadly substance functions if it cannot be injected by the frog. It is believed that the toxin exists primarily to make the frogs unpalatable. Dendrobatids are considered a classic example of a biological principle known as aposomatic, or warning, coloration: a species that is distasteful or poisonous will have an increased chance of survival if it advertises its toxicity with distinct markings. Since a biologist's greatest love is firsthand information to support a theory, tests have been conducted on these frogs to determine their palatability. At least one biologist has discovered that *Phyllobates* should not be considered a new variety of frog legs; after placing one on his tongue, he reported a numbness and tightening of his throat. It is now known that had a more toxic species been selected, his taste test could have been fatal.

The espavel was 120 feet tall, and like most trees in virgin jungles, it lacked lower branches. The highest limbs were not visible, and I knew that blindly shooting a line into the crown might lead to a dangerous situation—the unseen branch could break once I was high above the ground. This happened to me once, and fortunately I fell into a river. Reaching the canopy demanded a strategy, much like planning an assault on a mountain. This particular climb would be accomplished in two stages. The first stage would take me to the lowest of the upper limbs, where there would be a better view of the crown.

I loosened the drawstrings of my backpack and began unloading two nine-millimeter climbing ropes from the upper compartment. The middle compartment held two waterproof gas-mask bags containing camera gear, and the lower section held a spool of fishing line, gloves, insect repellent, climbing hardware, glassine envelopes for insect specimens, collapsible collecting nets, a hard hat, nylon cord, arrows, and a parachute harness made of seat-belt material. The total weight of this equipment was over sixty pounds.

I aimed the crossbow with my right arm, held the spool of fishing line in my left, and shot. The arrow jumped skyward and line whirred from the spool. Almost instantly I put pressure on the line with my thumb to slow the arrow so it would arch over a good-sized branch about sixty feet high, but the shot went astray. The second try was perfect and the arrow fell back to the ground, pulling additional line from the spool.

The fishing line was not strong enough to lift the climbing rope so it had to be replaced with two-hundred-pound-test nylon cord. The danger in this operation was that the fishing line might slip into a groove of the bark. Pulling the cord into place would then be impossible. Fortunately luck was with me, and within a half hour I had the climbing rope up and over the limb. This may sound easy, but the pitfalls are numerous and can lead to the loss of an entire morning's work.

Once the rope was draped over the limb, I tied one end to a secure anchor, a tree one foot in diameter, using a "gripping" bowline knot. Developing new knots—knots new at least to me—without first testing them is risky business, and I tied several additional half hitches behind the bowline for mental well-being.

The harness went on like a coat, with a strap over each shoulder while waist and leg straps secured it to the body. It had wider straps than those found on mountaineering harnesses traditionally used for rope climbing. The latter weigh less but are more apt to cut one's circulation during long hours of quiet observation.

I attached an ascender to the rope and used a carabiner to connect my harness to the ascender. Foot stirrups hung from a second ascender, which was placed on the rope below the first. Ascenders clamp a rope when weight is applied and will move freely up and down when unweighted.

I began taking slack from the rope by putting one foot in a stirrup and pushing it to the ground. Then I lifted the harness ascender as high as I could reach. The rope now had a slight tension and it pulled up lightly on my harness. I slid the stirrup ascender up to just below the harness ascender and repeated the move; tightening the rope was like stretching a large rubber band. The result gave my body a simulated weightlessness comparable in some respects to what one would experience on the moon. A normal walking step sent me sailing. My reflexes were not used to this "weightlessness" and I bounced like a yo-yo, my butt crushing ground plants and my torso striking the trunk. Ants swarmed with the onslaught, but since my methods allowed me to move away from the trunk, I was able to avoid bites and stings.

Doyly observed my preparations while contending with a cloud of mosquitoes. I waved him over so he could hang from the rope with me, making sure he understood that we were testing the limb to see if it would hold our combined weight. It was a serious matter because if the limb broke, it could have killed us both. He clutched the back of my harness, pulling us to the ground, then he let go so I could climb up a few feet. I did this by alternately standing in the stirrups, then sitting back in the harness while sliding the ascenders up the rope. The motion was reminiscent of a giant inchworm.

We continued tightening the rope until we were suspended off the ground. For several minutes we listened for the slightest sound of wood snapping under the load. We heard nothing so Doyly dropped free from the harness and I shot up like an aircraft that has discarded ballast.

I had imagined that tropical tree climbing would have been somewhat like playing tennis, physical and clean, but this idea was quickly dispelled when at fifteen feet I had to hack through obstructing branches with a machete. Dirt and organic material resembling wet coffee grounds rained onto my clothing, leaving stains and a disagreeable odor.

The espavel would be the dirtiest tree I ever climbed, but compared to North American trees, all tropical trees are grimy. Liverworts, mosses, ferns, and many other epiphytes grow on the vertical surfaces of trunks and the upper sides of limbs. Their roots twist along bark grooves to secure a footing and to search for nutrients, yet they do not become parasites on the tree. Eventually the roots form a mat that can become a foot or more thick. The mat in turn traps falling particles that accumulate and eventually decompose into a nutrient-rich humus that supports many organisms. Humus on limbs is often even thicker than the rapidly decomposing layer on the ground. Climbing disturbs this material, causing a rain of moist particles.

I thrashed at branches, trying to enlarge the opening and still avoid the grime, a hopeless and awkward task. I watched with horror as the blade rebounded from a branch straight into the rope. Luckily it left only a small nick. I immediately gave up that practice.

Waterfall in Costa Rican jungle.

Helicopter damselfly of understory.

Lizard.

Red bird-dispersed seeds of understory
vine *Siparuna*.

Large baseball-sized seed of canopy tree
Carapa provides food stores for seedling
to become established in the dark understory.

Bats, such as this rare *Ectophyllo alba*, are very important dispersers and pollinators of jungle plants.

A poison-dart frog, *Dendrobates pumilio*, carrying a tadpole.

A formidable ground snake, a five-foot-long fer-de-lance eating a rat.

MID-ZONE LIFE

Epiphytes adorn the trunk of a silk cotton tree and provide cover for numerous animals.

Centipede from tree trunk.

The forest roof forms a canyon of leaves above a swamp.

Above the trimmed branches the ground became obscured and a new collection of plants with closer affinities to the forest's upper levels colonized the available perches. A monstera with large leaves clung to a nearby trunk. Anthuriums and bromeliads grew like tiny bushes on trunks and limbs or anywhere else they could take hold. A bromeliad cradled in the loop of a long, dangling, woody vine swayed gently from motion telegraphed down the vine's hundred-foot length; this was evidence that a breeze buffeted the forest's roof.

I was reminded of scuba diving in southern California kelp beds. Halfway to the ocean floor the kelp became a floating forest lacking ground and sky that pulsed as waves passed far overhead. The flimsy stems supported a profusion of leaves in long columns that provided homes for all kinds of fish, crabs, starfish, and other sea organisms. Buoyant bubbles made by hollow expansions of each leaf held the columns afloat while they reached for the indiscernible surface. Like kelp, the treetops also seemed suspended. Crowns were often seemingly oversized for their trunks; one large sphere of leaves balanced on a tall, lanky trunk that threatened to collapse under the stress.

At twenty-five feet the air became fresher due to a light breeze from the canopy. In the forest's lower layers the relative humidity hovers between 90 and 100 percent around the clock; in contrast, the canopy's relative humidity can be as low as 60 percent at midday. Sweat evaporated from my clothing as I rose into the drier air, a welcome cooling that lifted the oppressiveness of the damp, dark forest floor.

Months of anticipation became focused on those moments. I wanted to see a profound interaction of jungle life such as a scarlet macaw feeding fledglings, or a climbing snake taking prey. However, my first taste of canopy animal life was an annoying cloud of eighth-of-an-inch-long, brown sweat bees that became more numerous by the minute. These canopy insects crawled up my sleeves, down my neck, and into my eyes in a merciless quest for moisture and possibly salt. A few minutes of their company would make anyone frantic, and I hurriedly draped insect netting from my hard hat.

I tugged at a vine to see if a snake had taken refuge in the intertwined roots. Beige tendrils, which held the vine firmly to the trunk's surface, pulled free and released a miniature avalanche of debris that pattered to the ground. Insects of many families scurried to the safety of adjacent vines; a complete ecosystem was attached to the trunk's vertical surface.

Three feet higher, the tree was shedding a plate-sized piece of bark under which a salamander, a frog, or numerous other species could be hiding. I prepared my camera and pulled gently at the bark, lifting it millimeter by millimeter.

Suddenly, like a horrible jack-in-the-box, a six-inch-long scorpion leapt from the enclosure onto my glove. Scorpions have a poisonous sting that ranges from being mildly toxic, like a bee sting, to deadly. Where this species fit within that range probably no one knew, and I did not want to find out. The creature was frantically searching for a new shelter and the closest was the flared back of my work glove. I shook my hand in reflex and sent the scorpion on a long arc toward Doyly, who watched with an amused "I told you so" expression. During its fall, the scorpion hooked a leaf and disappeared.

Following that episode, I looked for sedate, nonaggressive organisms. On my left, ten feet out of reach, rested a beautiful yellow orchid. Using both legs, I pushed from the trunk and swung out like a pendulum, catching a branch near the flower. Rootlike tendrils, structures used for anchorage by many arboreal plants, clutched the remains of a small branch that had once held the orchid in the canopy. Being caught by branches during its fall may have saved it from a slow death in the forest basement, but would it escape another kind of death? The pollinators of the bright upper layers might not descend to service plants of the forest's depths.

I swung back, striking the trunk with my feet, which to my surprise, resonated like a drum. I kicked the tree with the toe of my boot several more times. The deep-sounding thuds indicated that the tree was quite hollow.

Hollow trees are not necessarily weak nor are they usually dead. The living tissue of a tree is contained in an outer ring called the "vascular cambium," where growth takes place. The central wood, known as the heartwood, is dead. Many giant sequoias, the largest trees in the world, are both hollow and very much alive. There is a catch, however, to the strength of hollow trees. Although a hollow cylinder of any uniform material can be as strong as a solid cylindrical bar, this calculation assumes a perfect cylindrical shape, which is a situation rarely, if ever, found in rotting trees. I decided against more pendulum swings and inched along to my destination.

The tree trunk swelled to a dozen feet in diameter forty feet above ground where two stout limbs branched out from either side of the main trunk. The limbs reached high into the upper canopy, but the trunk ended after an additional ten feet as a jagged snag. From a distance the tree's features resembled a long, headless neck between two upraised arms. I found that I was hanging from a scrawny-looking branch that grew from the top of the snag. I climbed until the rope became embedded in a thick layer of moss through which the ascenders would not advance. This was an arm's length away from the snag's rim. Given earlier circumstances, I was naturally reluctant to take a handhold without first inspecting for animals. Since that was impossible, I whipped the area with a length of nylon strap, hoping to dispel any residents. I had not considered that a good lashing might cause an animal to become annoyed.

I gripped the rim with both hands and struggled for a foothold. Peering over the rim, I was surprised to find that the trunk was a shell, having a cylindrical hole slightly less than three feet in diameter. I struggled to the top where foul air wafted from the neck's open throat.

My attention was drawn to a buzzing sound from overhead. A large black bee was at the flowers of a melastome bush. This bush was growing on the surface of the tree as an epiphyte, but like all epiphytes it was not a parasite, such as mistletoe, whose roots invade living tissues for nutrients. I was fascinated by the bee and the flowers it visited, and I was reasonably certain this was the first time anyone had seen the animal responsible for this plant's reproduction. When the bee visited flowers its thorax vibrated and shook pollen onto its body. The anthers, a flower part for holding pollen, were designed like tiny saltshakers. These were the flowers I had seen scattered about the ground.

A high-pitched squeak came from the opening, and I glanced down in time to see a pink petal drifting into the tree's depths. I squatted, resting my right hand on the moss of the opposite rim for support, and saw gray forms fluttering deep within the entrance. A rootlike obstruction four feet into the cavity kept the lower passage enshrouded in darkness. More squeaking emanated from the enclosure below the obstruction, and as my eyes adjusted I saw a species of light-tolerant bat, *Saccopteryx bilineata*. This species roosts near the entrance to hollows or even on the underside of limbs; my presence had disturbed them.

That ended my first day in this giant tree. I would return several times and experience many different adventures—some more harrowing than others. By far the worst incident occurred in the summer of 1976, when I squatted in the identical spot at the entrance to this hollow tree and watched what I thought to be a clump of moss transform into a coiled eyelash viper, *Bothrops schlegelii*. Its large head was less than a half inch from my hand. Adrenaline exploded into my veins and I jumped back and fell a few feet to a jarring halt. I hung there for several minutes collecting my senses, then checked my equipment to see if any cameras had been damaged.

The eyelash viper is an arboreal pit viper known for exceptionally toxic venom that rapidly immobilizes its prey. The snake's habit of resting off the ground where it can easily strike at the upper body makes it a fearsome animal. In Costa Rica alone the eyelash viper is responsible for three to six deaths per year.

I was compelled to photograph the eyelash viper, but to take a clear shot I had to move some anthurium leaves aside. The snake showed no sign of life. Its lidless eyes were unmoving yellow jewels implanted in a jade body, a gargoyle guarding the hollow's entrance.

Creatures

in a Wooden Cavern

I SPENT the next day looking
around Rincon. It was built on a
two-hundred-yard-wide strip of land, an alluvium sandwiched between a steep hill and the bay. Houses on low stilts lined the base of
the hill. The stilts, by Rich's account, are to protect the houses from
rain, which in an occasional downpour flows from the slope in sheets
many inches deep.

I hiked up the hill into a thicket of second growth that contained, among other things, banana and papaya trees. The coati I
had met was also there, shoving his flexible nose through a rotting
limb as he rooted for food.

The only ripe fruit was on a banana tree that stood over fifteen
feet tall. The banana tree is really not a tree but a gigantic vegetable
with a stalk only a little tougher than celery. Certain that it would
topple under my weight, I went back to the office to inquire about
how bananas were harvested. To my surprise, I was told to cut the
tree down; that was the way it was done on plantations. In fact,

plantation trees are cultivated to be small, so that bunches do not become damaged when they fall. Armed with a machete, I walked back up the hill and severed the trunk with two whacks. Many bananas were mashed in the fall but dozens were in perfect condition.

Banana bunches are not light—the one I cut weighed about fifty pounds. It was a struggle to get it onto my shoulders, and the bananas shook with each step down the grade, causing many creatures living in the bunch to panic; frightened cockroaches and spiders scrambled from dark crevices and used my head as a springboard to safety. Banana workers are occasionally bitten by poisonous snakes in this way.

I hung the bananas from a beam beneath the elevated first floor of my cabin. This was supposed to keep animals off them, though in practice ants find the cord. Other insects must be kept away with a screened closet, which I didn't have. I went upstairs to wash and found the front door ajar. Although the door had no lock, I thought it had been closed. Scuffling noises came from inside, followed by the sound of crinkling paper. "What luck," I thought, "the company supplies a maid." However, upon entering the room, I found an entirely different situation to be at hand. An intruder was in the act of ransacking my belongings. Food packages and gear were strewn everywhere, and the culprit had his head completely inside the chocolate almonds bag as he pushed it across the floor.

Furious, I unsheathed my machete, charged into the room, and struck the coati on the hindquarters with the broad side of the blade. The coati's head emerged from the bag wearing a wicked smile of chocolate-covered teeth. I jumped back, impressed with the size of those teeth and the angry hiss accompanying the smile. The coati sped for the door with me in pursuit. I cornered him in the kitchen, again brandishing my machete. The animal returned the threat with another nasty hiss and I backed away giving him room to escape through the front door. Later I fashioned a coati-proof door latch of rope and nails to keep the beast away.

After two days Doyly and I were again at the wild cashew tree, he on the ground and I climbing toward the entrance. The brief hiatus had recharged my desire to explore the treetops, especially the hollow, which had been nagging at my curiosity. I was very reluctant to enter the hollow and spent much time convincing myself that a "real" biologist would not pass up such an opportunity; there could be little doubt that it offered the quickest initiation into the biology of jungle life.

I climbed slowly up the trunk in a manner resembling a tree sloth; each foot was a meditated advance. Either there were no concealed animals or I didn't see them.

Seeing, however, is not just looking at something. It is a complex process beginning with an image cast by the eye's lens onto the retina and ending with the brain's interpretation of the signals coming through the optic nerve. How we interpret what we see is strongly influenced by our experience and background. I had come from city streets and manicured parks that had left my visual perceptive powers weak from disuse. High natural risk would have helped to sharpen these powers but that element, too, is absent from civilized environments.

Doyly was agitated that I had again decided to climb the tree and it showed in the dark furrows of his face. Wisely, I had waited until we arrived at the espavel to tell him that I would be exploring the hollow. This was to avoid the risk of Rich meddling in my affairs, but it had placed Doyly in a difficult position. Rich had entrusted him with my safety, and even I did not know how he could help if I ran into a problem.

It was possible that the hollow would become gradually narrower, like a glacial crevasse; if that was the case, even a short fall could cause me to become wedged between the walls. Ice climbers occasionally die that way. My worry, however, was becoming helpless amid a throng of bizarre creatures. I tied my rope tightly to a limb near the mouth of the hollow, taking care that it would not slip and drop me into the fissure.

With my first step into the hollow, I met the obstruction that bisected the opening. I tested to see if it would hold my weight, then crouched to examine the underside. Heavy, stench-laden air rose up the passage and nearly overpowered me. Fortunately, the olfactory sense habituates quickly, even to powerful odors.

The beam of my headlamp reached beyond the obstruction down into a shaft, which was like a natural smokestack, but the light did not penetrate the darkness. To determine the depth, I took a coin from my pocket and dropped it into the void. It took about two seconds to fall, a figure that plugged nicely into a Newtonian formula hammered into my memory over years of higher education. What an opportunity! How often are we able to use knowledge tortured into us during college?

The calculation was simple: the depth of a hole is equal to one half the acceleration of gravity (thirty-two feet per second squared) multiplied by the time it took the coin to fall (two seconds) squared, or four times sixteen feet, or sixty-four feet. Sixty-four feet had to be an overestimate because the ground was only fifty feet below. Accurate timing would have led to a precise measure of depth, though the estimate was close enough to establish that the hollow went deep into the gigantic trunk.

The underside of the obstruction had not been fully visible, so while I crept through the narrow opening trying to avoid the dirty walls, I was also expecting a few surprises. The only creatures I noticed were the small colony of *Saccopteryx* bats roosting on the near part of the shaft and a swarm of gnats that waded daintily in a thin film of goo on the interior surface.

To protect myself, I had covered every inch of my body with clothing, which would unavoidably make me hot in the warm environment of the hollow. I wore an insect net over my hard hat and face; gloves that extended over my long-sleeved shirt and my denim pants were tucked into the tops of my Vietnam War-style jungle boots.

I swung over the opening between the wall and obstruction while dangling in the harness. To enter without rubbing against the enclosure required that I descend in small increments in a vertical, or standing, position while controlling my swing and placing my toes against the enclosure. This startled the gnats, which had been feasting on the wall, and they rose in a cloud around me.

Transition into the vertical shaft sparked a growing dread. On the underside of the obstruction a few inches away, a scorpion rested impassively. I took a bag from a pocket and imprisoned the animal until I was finished exploring the tree. Bats had been in the air since I entered the hollow, and they became overwrought with the light beam. They crashed into me on their kamikaze flight to escape. At the height of this frenzy I inhaled a gnat that had found its way under the insect net. I spit in disgust, knowing that the animal had thrived in filth.

In the 80 degree temperature and 100 percent humidity, moisture rose from my soaked clothes and condensed into swirls of mist. I sat motionless for a time to cool off, and the *Saccopteryx* settled on the walls above the obstacle waiting to return to the comfort of their foul roost.

Below, the walls faded into black nothingness, and overhead the forest had become a distant world. The floor of the hollow was not visible. This was a clue to what lay below, but at the time my attention was given to a fit of claustrophobic anxiety. I increased my speed, hoping to end the adventure quickly.

Rather than narrowing, the shaft abruptly opened into a gigantic wooden grotto seven feet below the obstacle. Dangling in space at the roof of a cavernous enclosure quickly brought my claustrophobia to an end. The cylindrical chamber was remarkably like a limestone cave. It dropped for forty feet, narrowing as a waist does, and then broadened again, terminating at a black earth floor.

The ceiling had two additional projections extending into the major limbs. One, like the entrance, vented into the jungle, but the opening was blocked on the outside by the melastome bush and a mass of other epiphytes. I swept my light beam into the other hollow limb, and out of its farthest reaches came a din of screeching that resounded throughout the main cavern. I had disturbed a colony of hundreds of leaf-nosed bats, most of which were a fruit-eating species, *Phyllostomous discolor*. Several fell from the roof and circled around without striking me, as if in reconnaissance. Soon they rejoined their kin in the cul-de-sac, which was totally protected from weather, light, and predators.

Pure white plate fungi grew from the wall near the mouth of the cul-de-sac. To look at them closer, I pushed off the wall and grabbed a knob of wood hanging from the ceiling like a stalactite. Each plate protected a colony of small leafhoppers, or homopterans, ranging from immature to adult stages. Several fungi, of a type I had never seen before, hung from the same plates like miniature chandeliers. Later, when I left the cavern, I collected specimens of this fungus for close inspection and photography but, unfortunately, after only a few minutes away from the cavern's protective environment, the specimens dissolved into fluid.

Fungi, along with termites, wood-boring beetles, and other organisms had excavated and continued to excavate the arboreal cavern. In one place where my boot had scraped the wall, a two-inch section of a termite colony's tunnel was opened. Soldiers quickly guarded the damaged corridor to protect a line of workers from would-be attackers.

The many animals at the top of the enclosure made me wonder what lived in the four-story volume below. I rappelled down the rope using special hardware, which is a way to descend by letting gravity do the work. One's rate of descent can be easily controlled with speeds ranging from a thrilling "free-fall" to a pace of an inch at a time. I descended slowly, hunting for life.

Parts of the wall were very smooth, with fine wood-grain patterns, though much of the surface was dripping with the same humuslike material held in epiphyte roots on the outside of the tree. Crickets an inch and a half long walked in the muck as blind men, their six- to eight-inch antennae touching the surroundings in search of food and aggressors.

An incubus of the insect world sat in a dark depression several feet below the crickets. Known as an amblypygid, or whip scorpion, this grotesque beast had skinny legs that could have enveloped my hand. Amblypygids, exclusively tropical animals, lurk in cracks, under bark, and in other protected places until the sun sets when they emerge to stalk unwary prey on limbs and trunks. Those inside the tree, however, probably seldom ventured outside.

The amblypygid waited motionless while feeling for prey with long antennae-like front legs that swept over a large radius. Victims die a cruel death, for an amblypygid is a living incarnation of the iron maiden, a medieval torture device. Unlike scorpions, amblypygids are not poisonous, but next to the mouth are two modified legs, or pseudo-jaws, that have rows of needle-sharp spines for skewering prey. Often, prey remains alive while being slowly ingested.

Even ferocious amblypygids have their nemesis. A bud of white fungus blossomed from a walking leg of one individual. The fungus would ultimately consume the animal, but until then the whip scorpion would remain a potent foe for any small creature of the hollow.

At twenty feet above the ground I began to pass a group of large cockroaches (*Blaberus giganteus*), the adults being about three inches long. These were attractive in appearance for roaches, and one could almost imagine a face gazing up through layers of translucent wings, a feature that has given this species the common name "cockroach of the divine face." There were dozens of adults, all sitting, as sea gulls on a beach, evenly spaced and facing upward. Immature jet-black roaches also formed part of the aggregation that, undoubtedly, feasted upon the filth stuck to the wall.

Large roaches were not new to me because as a child I lived in southern Arizona, an area known locally for its record-breaking roaches. Those in the tree, however, made the big "water beetles" that infested Arizona homes seem like midgets.

I tried to collect a large adult but it leapt from the wall, flew onto the net in front of my face, then disappeared behind my head. It dodged my wild slaps by careening repeatedly over my shoulders, head, and chest. On one of these circuits I caught the roach, but strong claws on each of its six feet clung firmly to my shirt. Pulling hard at the insect's natural wrapper would only have added to the mess accumulating on my clothes so I let go and persuaded the roach, with several hard swats from my glove, to return to the wall.

I came to a stop three feet above the ground and carefully inspected it for bushmasters. Though nothing seemed amiss, I did not descend but instead turned off the headlamp to "see" the hollow from the perspective of its inhabitants. This could only be a simulated perspective since each organism lives in a world nearly impossible to imagine. Without light I was blind, not unlike the crickets and whip scorpions; the rope was my safety. I hung there wondering what might venture into the hollow now that it was again dark.

After many minutes I began to see vague forms. Turns and bends of wood and mottled color patterns appeared on the wall's surface. The source of light was the entrance far above, which looked like the full moon in a midnight sky. Ironically, this was daytime in that Stygian realm. Perhaps at some time during the tropical sun's annual course, bright rays pierced the hollow.

I then examined the cavern with my light and was astonished to find a small, ratlike mammal with blond fur frozen in the beam. The animal sat on a wooden shelf a couple of feet above the floor. I descended to look at it more closely, taking photographs along the way. The electronic flash repeatedly lit the interior, but to my amazement, the rodent did not move. When I was an arm's length away I reached out and nudged the animal in the ribs with my index finger. It did not run but merely tried to avoid my finger by arching its back.

The rat was really not a rat at all, but a very interesting mammal relatively common in South and Central America. It was a rat opossum, which belongs to the primitive pouched mammals or marsupials. Unlike North American opossums, the rat opossum has lost its pouch over the millennia. Its diet consists of fruits and insects, and except for size and general appearance, rat opossums are quite different from rats.

What was the opossum doing in the hollow tree? It may have been feasting on the abundance of insects. However, another side to their gourmet disposition should be told. Paul Abravaya, a biologist who once visited the tree with me, spent considerable time in Brazil where he was able to observe the behavior of captive rat opossums. He finds them ferociously aggressive toward other small mammals; one captive animal overpowered and ate bats that were placed in its cage. Whether rat opossums eat bats in the wild is not known, but if they do, situations like the hollow tree would give them ample opportunity.

I noticed a movement on the floor and flashed my light in that direction, catching the bright eye-shine of a good-sized animal. It was the largest frog in Central America (*Leptodactylus pentadactylus*). This, too, is an aggressive animal that has been known to eat snakes up to a half yard long. I lunged to catch the frog but it jumped beneath a ledge. Stooping to capture the trapped animal, I discovered to my surprise that an arm of the hollow extended far into the root. Ten feet into the subterranean corridor, the frog ducked behind a bend.

Around the rim of the floor, a ring of corridors radiated away from the hollow as spokes of a wheel. The frog's escape corridor was marked by numerous footprints showing that it was a heavily used path, one that communicated with the forest. A couple of the other "subways" were also routes of travel to and from the forest, suggesting that the hollow and its organisms were attractive to a variety of jungle-floor animals. I found it amusing that canopy exploration had ultimately deposited me beneath the forest.

While I was exploring the roots, the rat opossum had quietly vanished down one of the subterranean passages. Sitting alone and reflecting in that strange place made it seem like a fairy-tale world straight from Lewis Carroll's *Alice in Wonderland*. I had just met a "door mouse" of refined disposition and a frog with glowing eyes who beckoned me to follow him through an underground passage. I might have been tempted to try a mushroom to make myself shrink, except that a tiny human would have been no match for the hollow's hungry inhabitants.

Photography within the tree was extremely difficult. Even minor exertion in the 100 percent humidity caused mist from sweat to fog my camera lenses. There was another problem: every time a flash went off the bats became excited. They nervously released a fine spray and soft pellets that splattered against my hard hat. I had to quickly cover my camera after every shot.

One would have expected months and years of raining guano to accumulate into a pile several feet deep, but when I stepped onto the ground my feet sank only slightly. I lifted a handful of the earth, which was like the material in the roots of outside plants, but much richer. Cupped in my palm was a thriving sea of stercoricolous insect larvae: immature beetles, roaches, and other insects. These literally poured from my glove and disappeared into the guano sea as quickly as fish hitting water.

Guano was the lifeblood of the hollow-tree community. The tiny scavengers and other organisms near the bottom of the energy pyramid flourished and became the cornerstones of a diverse predatory community. Over a complete year the hollow was probably visited by a vital cross section of jungle life, making it a natural laboratory and one of the best possible locations to conduct studies of many nocturnal forms, organisms that would be difficult or impossible to observe and study elsewhere.

Bats, the source of the guano, dispersed at night into the forest to find food. These were fruit-eating bats, unlike the almost exclusively insectivorous bats of temperate regions. Their small size and need for high body temperatures during flight demand countless visitations to trees, shrubs, and epiphytes to fulfill their energetic needs, and in turn they sow the seeds of much jungle plant life and enrich the hollow with their waste.

Bats are the most important tropical rain forest mammals. The warm climate and availability of a wide variety of fruit and nectar, as well as insects, have fostered the existence of numerous species. For example, in Costa Rica alone there are 103 species of bats while in all of North America there are only forty species.

I dug at the floor, exposing more beetles and finally, the ground. The tree did not have a wooden bottom so guano fell directly on earth. The significance of that observation was far-reaching, for the nutrients that left the guano found their way into the underlying soil where they probably were used by the espavel.

The tree no doubt benefited from the bats, and the bats benefited from housing supplied by the tree in a sort of mutualism. I say "sort of mutualism" because the word *mutualism* is often reserved to describe a relationship between two organisms that benefit both and is necessary for each to survive. Such a tight mutualism did not exist between the espavel and its bats since both species could live without the other. But at least the tree and the bats existed in a cooperative environment.

Since tropical soils are typically nutrient-poor, and hollows attract many forms of nutrient-producing organisms, one might expect that hollowness in the espavel may have been an advantage. I explored the area surrounding Rincon and found that, indeed, most of the larger espavel trees were hollow, showing that this species has a tendency to lose its heartwood.

Even if the long-term benefits of being hollow are questionable, it seems likely that guano would have given the tree increased vitality and, at least in the short term, an advantage over other trees in meeting nutrient demands. If the espavel lived a normal life span, this would translate into a greater number of surviving offspring, a selective force for the development of a mutualism between the tree and bats. If that were true, then I had stumbled onto a relationship between mammals and trees that had not been seen before.

I climbed a few feet above the floor and turned off the light, again hoping to draw additional animals to the hollow. After several minutes I became aware of slight changes in the natural light level within the cavern. For a moment I thought it was my eyes adjusting to the darkness, but I soon realized that the phenomenon was due to an opening in the opposite wall. Very weak and wavering light came through a small, cone-shaped hole three feet above the floor. In effect, the hole and near pitch-black cavern constituted a crude optical device. The hole acted as a lens to cast a fuzzy image of the outside world onto the wall. In some urban parks buildings have been similarly constructed for watching outside events projected onto a screen; they are called camera obscuras.

A weak, upside-down image of Doyly was projected onto the opposite wall. I looked through the opening and saw him pacing at the foot of the tree, undoubtedly worried about the fact that he had not heard from me for quite a while. I looked at my watch: five hours had passed, longer than it had seemed.

I screamed through the hole as loudly as possible to get Doyly's attention, but my cries were totally muted by the cavern. It was then that the extent of my isolation from the safe outside world became very real. The rope, my only connection with civilization, rose to a very distant tiny exit, and I wondered what would happen if somehow it became untied.

The teeming sea of insects at my feet, the unpleasant atmosphere, scorpions, bats, roaches, hours of confinement, and my distressed companion combined to make me long to be in the forest's clean, bright air. The climb was necessarily slow, and as I approached the glowing exit I knew that I had had a unique experience of natural history, an invaluable initiation into the unusual intricacies of treetop life.

That was my trip in 1974. In 1982, as the ferry carried Rafa and me closer to the Osa, my heart gradually sank. The hills of forest were fighting a losing battle against man. Large gaps had been cleared for farming, which together with chunks of remaining forest gave the countryside a checkerboard appearance. Possibly the hollow tree had been spared, but since it stood on choice land that seemed unlikely.

In Puerto Jimenez, Rafa and I rented a taxi for the trip to Rincon, about ten miles away. Rafa's presence had no effect on the fare; since I was an American, we were gouged for twice the going rate. It was already 10 A.M. so we would have to travel quickly and have some phenomenal luck in order to reach Rincon, see the tree, and return to catch the five o'clock ferry that left Puerto Jimenez for Golfito.

November is normally a terrible time to visit the Osa because it is the worst month of the rainy season. Fortunately, 1982 was an unusually dry year, which made it possible to drive to the hollow tree. The road crossed five rivers before reaching the airstrip, and if all went well the ride would take a half hour.

The river crossings held substantial amounts of water, which Angel, our driver, bravely negotiated. Each time we dove dolphin-like into water, steam passed through rust holes of the engine compartment and flooded the cab. We had our own little sauna in the tropical heat.

I asked Angel why he didn't drive more slowly through the rivers. He looked back with a serious expression while stomping his foot up and down on the brake pedal. *"No hay freno!"* he said; we had no brakes.

Everywhere were recent clearings, and not only Costa Ricans were in the act of subduing the jungle. Europeans and Americans were also swinging axes against Osa's trees in a last-gasp effort of the human species to take all the earth's land for themselves. I knew that in the future I would see green pastures, cattle, and erosion. And in not too many additional years there would be injured land with no forests, no macaws, no monkeys, no snakes, no beauty anywhere, only a multitude of shanties and potbellied children.

The people carried smiles on their faces, smiles of plenty and hope. With their work and their dreams they reached for prosperity, but in the future their hands would not even grasp good earth.

Angel had his tiny bit of the future in me, and as we bounced down the road it felt as though destiny would step in to part our company. On the incline toward our final crossing I sensed trouble: the current looked deeper and faster than the previous streams. When the taxi plunged into the river, water splashed into the compartment, then slowly rose above the floorboards. The vehicle came to a stop but the engine was alive, bellowing its fate in rising bubbles of exhaust. The tires scraped ineffectually for a bite at loose gravel. I threw my backpack onto the roof to keep it dry and jumped into waist-deep water to give a helping hand, but the engine soon died. The pickup was like an elephant sinking into a mudhole.

A threatening cloud hung over the hills that fed the stream. If the storm came, the taxi would be washed into Golfo Dulce, ending Angel's parasitic career. At this point the fare could only escalate, as a tractor would be needed for the rescue. With this in mind, I decided it was time to depart, so I paid Angel for taking us as far as the river and told him I might be back but not to wait. I then caught up with Rafa, who had already begun walking the three remaining miles to the airport.

My hopes waxed and waned as we passed new clearings and surviving pieces of forest. Gone were the forests that had once touched limb tips above the road. We passed a thatched-roof shack with an ax leaning against a wall, its edge honed and glimmering from recent use. Sun beat down on land with the distinctively oppressive heat of pasture.

The espavel, if it had survived the onslaught, stood at the base of a small foothill below a mountain that was still covered with trees. Rafa told me that when the land had been abandoned by the logging company, squatters drifted in. The government had declared the forest on the hollow tree's side of the airstrip a reserve and removed the squatters, but only after much damage had been done. There was no way of knowing if the tree still stood.

Near a clearing we saw two king vultures sitting on a limb, their scarlet heads and pure white bibs sharply defined against the green of tree crowns. King vultures are rare and thought to be nearing extinction.

I was overcome by sorrow as we set out to cross the Agua Buena. Blue sky shone through the trees on the creek's far bank. The alluvial plain where the tree once stood had been cleared and was overgrown with dense, nearly impenetrable brush. Merely walking to the site would be difficult, but I needed to see the espavel, even if all that remained was a rotten stump.

Long ago I cried about the death of jungles but have since come to accept that fate. The forces at work are tremendous. They are human, economic, and political. And there is a broader scale to the problem, one which places the current situation in perspective. From the time life began in a primeval sea, the earth's biological face has been constantly changing. Consecutive waves of extinction have dealt blow after blow to existing life forms. Over 99 percent of all the species that have ever lived are now extinct. It would appear that tropical forests will follow the same route.

Rafa and I waded downstream to the bend where the trail

began. The trail was gone. It had been choked by a nasty tangle of plant life that reclaims recently cut forest. This is the sort of jungle described by most popular writers, a thick and virtually impassable growth, the scab on a forest wound.

The remainder of the search was a sickening journey. I wielded my machete as Doyly had done years before. I was in the lead and alert for vipers, but obsessed with what lay ahead. Each yard took us by a fallen jungle lord, and from beneath their prostrate corpses sprang new shoots of hope. Jungle life fought to survive; dendrobatids still hopped through the litter; ants were everywhere, and small tree seedlings struggled to win their place in the regenerating forest. Left to itself, in a few decades the jungle would once again be beautiful, and in several centuries it would become an "untouched" rain forest.

Each foot had to be cleared for passage. Debris rained on our unprotected heads. We parted cobwebs with our hands and I searched for signs that we were on the correct course. Then off to my left I saw an old friend. Miraculously, the clear cutting had stopped twenty yards short of the espavel's base. All around, sharp-eyed loggers had taken the best trees for wood. Hollowness had extended the espavel's ultimate sentence.

We approached the tree; it seemed healthy and the vines may have been even denser. Perhaps this was due to the removal of adjacent trees, which let more light through to the forest floor. There was a hole at the base of the tree that had not been there before. The musty smell of bat guano still hung in the air. To explore the hollow would have taken a full day, time that we did not have. Fallen leaves in the passage were matted down from animal traffic. Mammals were probably exploiting the hollow.

The harsh screeching of red-lored and orange-chinned parrots bid us good-bye. Swifts moved constantly over the injured forest taking insects that effervesced off the canopy's flourishing upper surface. Perhaps the espavel and its complex community of life will survive many years, but more likely a flood of humanity will wash away any evidence of the untouched jungle, just as the Agua Buena erased my prints from its sandy banks.

Finca La Selva

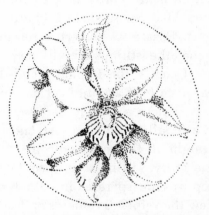

THE LOWLAND rain forest canopy
I have explored for the past ten
years lies in a region called the Sarapiqui, sixty miles north, as the
crow flies, of the capital, San José. To reach the jungle I usually take
the Rapido, a bus line whose name should in no way be correlated
with its performance. The journey entails a five-hour trip over unimproved rural roads that are steep, narrow, and covered with a regular succession of deep potholes. Frequent breakdowns typically add
hours to the travel time.

The only major town along the route is Alajuela, and like all
outlying towns, it radiates pastoral serenity. Alajuela has a delight-
fully alluring central square where one night a week visitors can
sit on benches and listen to live music played by Alajuela's own
philharmonic orchestra. Huge broad-leaf trees attract groups of
schoolchildren, shoppers, and lovers. Overhead limbs hold many
varieties of exquisite orchids and other airplants that add their own
fragrances and colors when in bloom. I am told by residents that

51

these trees offer concealment to a family of Perezosos, or tree sloths, and provide food for flocks of parrots that visit the square.

The road climbs gradually from the outskirts of Alajuela through a cool, high pass between Vulcan Poas and Vulcan Barba. From there it winds down precipitous terrain to a flat expanse of lowland jungle that once extended in a continuous blanket from the Yucatan Peninsula of Mexico to the Amazon Basin of South America. Poas is one of many national parks; Costa Rica has the highest percentage of land set aside for parks of any country in the world, including the United States. Cloudless days are rare on Poas, but when they occur the peak has stunning scenery of lowland jungle, an azure crater lake surrounded by cloud forest, and a sterile sister lake whose surface is often disturbed by huge gaseous eruptions. Poas is a powerful reminder that the geologic forces that shaped the isthmus are still very active.

Usually the Rapido plodded along the road without stopping except to load and unload passengers. However, when approaching a site where a vehicle had recently gone off a cliff, the bus would occasionally pull over. At one of these locations a bus had gone straight off the road and rolled several hundred yards to the bottom of a gully, killing seven people. For weeks afterward an additional stop was incorporated into the Rapido's itinerary so passengers could view the vehicle's remains and cast silent prayers.

Along this route the road traversed gorges hundreds of feet deep. Window seats were especially galvanic as the bus zigzagged down hairpin turns hugging the brink of many vertical cliffs. The ride was interspersed with exhilarating vistas of magnificent waterfalls, rivers, and virgin forests.

I often felt that traveling to and from the jungle was much more perilous than canopy work, and I have cast prayers myself in hopes of arriving safely. On one dark night while traveling through the same terrain, the bus lost its lights during a dense fog. I was accompanied by Paul Abravaya and a full load of petrified passengers. The road margins were indiscernible, but this did not deter the driver, who forged ahead with resolution. Unnerved, Paul and I quickly dug two flashlights from our bags, leaned out windows on either side of the bus, and lit the road as best we could. It would be difficult to find a slower ride packed with more excitement.

The scientific research station, called Finca La Selva, or The Jungle Farm, whose untouched jungle is the setting for the remainder of this book, is an hour and a half away from the volcanic foothills. During less opulent times, when Caribbean jungles were nearly continuous, Finca La Selva was a modest retreat having several buildings that included a dining room, kitchen facilities, and dormitories for researchers. As Caribbean jungles shrank, international interest in tropical studies increased, and the station has expanded to absorb the influx of scientists.

The new Ciudad La Selva, or The Jungle City, has all but abandoned its most picturesque tradition—the use of dugout canoes as transportation. The boats are relics from early Indian cultures now extinct in the area. Once the primary means of communication with Puerto Viejo, the nearest cow town, they have recently become outmoded. Now a gravel road dead-ends across from the station, and a hundred-thousand-dollar suspension footbridge has been erected over the Rio Puerto Viejo, giving direct access to thousands of acres of private jungle reserve.

My first visit to the station was in August of 1974, soon after discovering the hollow tree. Gary Stiles, of the University of Costa Rica, had told me that La Selva had some of the most fascinating canopy communities in Central or South America and that the trees were tall with huge trunks, the first limbs of which were seventy or eighty feet above ground. Many of these large trees would be literally covered with epiphytes and, he warned, treetop ants.

I departed the bus at the Monteverde, an open-air bar, restaurant, and motel in Puerto Viejo. In crude Spanish I asked Ramon, the proprietor, where the noontime boat to La Selva disembarked. To ask a question in a foreign language is one problem; understanding the answer is another. With the help of sign language, he was able to convey that the launch would "dock" at the end of a gravel road across from his restaurant.

I lugged my bags for several hundred yards to the end of the road and found that the landing was no more than a steep gravel grade into the river. While waiting for the boat I noticed a four-foot-long iguana (*Iguana iguana*) drowsing on a high limb. The species is second in size only to the huge predaceous monitor lizards of the

Lesser Sunda Islands. A row of spines down the length of an iguana's backbone has given them a formidable appearance and helped some to be cast as monsters in certain low-budget "horror" films.

In actuality iguanas are shy creatures that exist largely on a diet of tree leaves and fruit. Like cows, they spend much idle time digesting tough plant materials. Since lizards do not produce the metabolic heat that aids digestion, they can often be seen sunning themselves, putting solar energy to work.

Iguanas are called "*pollo de palo*," which means chicken of the tree. They are eaten throughout tropical America, and the taste of their meat lives up to the common name. The foregoing no doubt is one reason for the timidity of iguanas, an aspect of their behavior that I experienced once when I was trying to photograph a nesting pair of pale-billed woodpeckers.

I had placed a rope in a small tree and began to test its strength. My weight shook the tree and started an avalanche of debris that crashed like cannon balls into the river behind me. Thinking that a large limb would surely be following, I dove for safety. When all was quiet I glanced to see what had hit the river's surface, but nothing was there. Later, I told the story to a herpetologist who said that several large iguanas, anticipating trouble, must have plunged into the river and swam to its bottom to hide.

Across the road from the sunbathing iguana, a number of turkey vultures decorated the top of a tree by holding their wings, of five-foot span, in the sun to dry. A flock of hundreds of these birds sunning themselves is a memorable sight and has been said to resemble a "witches' sabbath."

Though the area was largely pasture, it had tantalizing reminders of a recent uncivilized era. There were oases of canopy life perched atop wooden pinnacles stretched to the limits of height. These trees, giant almendros (*Dipteryx panamensis*), stood isolated in fields; remnants of the primeval forest. Some, with trunks six feet in diameter, were as tall as a seventeen-story building. I was a novice climber with only the hollow tree under my belt; the trees of the Sarapiqui looked like the Himalayas.

The river's calm pools reflected the green of jungle fig trees that crowded its bank. Their falling fruit rippled its surface, then bobbed and floated to swifter currents; some of the figs disappeared in a boil of activity produced by large frugivorous fish. Elephant ears choked the roadside. The leaves of this herbaceous plant are the size of an umbrella, for which they can be used. A kingfisher sat on a snag reaching from the far bank, and butterflies flew near the water's surface.

The faint hum of an outboard came from far upriver. In minutes Rafael, the La Selva boatman, pulled a twenty-five-foot-long dugout canoe to the landing. *"Cómo está?"* he asked in the clearest, most perfect Spanish. "Fine," I answered in equally clear English.

The ride upriver had a few rough spots, which Rafael easily navigated. He knew the rapids and could read the currents for hidden snags, sand bars, and drifting logs. The forest lined the banks, and Rafael's knowledge of the wild river brought vivid visions of Mark Twain's *Life on the Mississippi.*

In Mark Twain's time the forest along the Mississippi was virtually intact. Since North America's forest was one of the largest expanses of forest on the earth, it seemed unconquerable; that pioneers would so swiftly bring the American ecosystem to its knees was unforeseen. Pioneers have not changed, and progress has turned on nature with a vengeance. Axes being too slow, man, the child of trees, has acquired new tools. Now with the help of petroleum, the blood of long-vanished jungles, chain saws attack the forest's feet. Clear cutting has swept across Central America and up the Amazon where forces of destruction have raised their ugly heads as never before. Immense but portable machines, themselves covering acres of land, are masticating the earth's forests into pulp. We are witnessing an epochal stage in the evolution of life; all over the world trees are being driven to extinction while crowds of humans take possession of the land.

Rafael signaled toward the bank, where a caiman quickly slid from a log and disappeared. Above the last set of rapids before arriving at La Selva the river became very calm and picturesque. Hundred-foot-tall trees with dangling vines and epiphytes draped over their branches formed a nearly complete umbrella over the river. Rafael slowed the engine and waved again. Three black river turtles were sunning on a log and they, too, slipped into the water.

Once when I was floating down the Puerto Viejo in a dugout canoe, I passed a beautiful yellow epiphytic orchid that was resting on a low branch. After some vigorous back-paddling, I was able to collect it for photography. Coincidentally, the plant held a spider that was strangely inactive. The reason for this inactivity became apparent once I began the photographic session. Soon the spider began moving, uncomfortably, then suddenly the spider's abdomen ripped open as it gave birth to a squirming, parasite, a nematode worm.

We arrived at La Selva's concrete landing platform. Steep steps and an iron railing led to the station, which was built on a high point overlooking the river to protect buildings from flooding. During a heavy downpour the Rio Puerto Viejo has been known to rise forty feet in only a few hours. Trails descend away from the research station in all directions to bridges or stream crossings, which become inundated. Although the buildings of La Selva remain dry, biologists working in the jungle have been caught unaware.

One of the worst floods of the area's history occurred in 1976. Researchers who were there at the time told horror stories about having to swim above submerged bridges in order to return to the station. Since floods also catch jungle animals unprepared, any swimming or wading was inevitably through a soup of desperate life. A dog-paddling biologist towing a soggy sack of plant leaves for study was an island of salvation for the drowning hordes of spiders, ants, frogs, legless lizards, snakes, and other frantic creatures. All buoyant objects became arks; floating leaves, sticks, and trees carried myriads of forlorn passengers to unknown destinies. Ground plants that were not yet submerged held a diverse assortment of small animals that had been herded by the rising water into small groups on topmost leaves. In one such flood I witnessed a spider, whose legs would span six inches, float by using her air-filled egg sac as a life preserver. Deluges are a boon to the fearless naturalist who does not mind wading in chest-deep water. More rare species can be seen in a few hours of flooding than during months of dry weather.

These floods have helped to disseminate the planet's life. Rivers everywhere carry creatures on oceanic journeys, a process of dispersal that has been called "sweepstakes" dispersal by George Gaylord Simpson. Imagine the millions of luckless organisms that are sent adrift by the tremendous outflow of the Amazon River during the rainy season: fresh water is detectable as far as two hundred miles out at sea. Survival for the marooned is unlikely; only a few will reach dry land again on a continent or an island, and it is rarer still that the migrants will reproduce and successfully colonize their new homes.

La Selva's accommodations were cleaner than the pension where I had stayed in Golfito, but there were no private rooms, a situation that has since changed. The upper story held a dormitory with numerous bunk beds; the mattresses were made from a heavy cotton fabric stretched between two parallel wood supports. Through heavy use, the cotton retained the general head and body impressions left by numerous visitors.

The dorm served scientists, students of tropical biology, and bird-watchers, many of whom complained bitterly of backaches. In recent years cotton fabric has been replaced by more comfortable foam mattresses. Foam holds moisture, which leads to mildew and its accompanying odor, but at least the beds do not rip when being shared.

Germans have a better word for jungle; they call it *Urwald*, which roughly translated means primeval forest, a forest with an enigmatic and foreboding history. La Selva was a human island embedded in that kind of jungle; from the dorm one could feel the *Urwald*. It stood just beyond the large screened windows, broadcasting its message in air perfumed with the scents of ripe fruits and sweet flowers. The *Urwald* pulled at me as the ocean calls to a mariner.

Within a half hour of my arrival I was hiking alone through the forest. La Selva's canopy was higher than the Osa's. It had immense trees whose tops were barely discernible behind the many levels of leaves. In these crowns were the aerial communities I wanted to explore.

On the near loop trail I stopped to watch a "river" of pink petals crossing the path. A two-inch-wide column of leaf-cutting ants was carrying flower parts to their subterranean nest, where they cultivated a special fungus. The nests are huge, holding up to five million workers, and entrances to the same nest can be separated by as much as half a football field. The relationship between the ants and fungus appears to be ancient. The fungus has lost the ability to produce spores and is totally dependent upon the ants for its existence and reproduction. Since spore development is essential for the classification of fungi, the kinship between the "ant fungus" and other fungi remains uncertain.

I followed the column for many yards into the sparse jungle undergrowth before finally arriving at the source: sweet-smelling flowers that had fallen in a fifty-foot radius around a trunk seven feet in diameter. Tens of thousands of flowers were on the ground and they had the delicate fragrance of sweet peas. The flowers had come from an almendro tree, a towering species belonging to the pea family.

Before me stood the largest pea stalk imaginable, larger even than that of "Jack and the Bean Stalk," though the almendro may not have been as tall. That fable comes to mind not only because it is an archetype of exploration and discovery, but also because it places symbolic importance upon a tree (Jack's bean stalk by botanical definition was a giant tree) as a vehicle to another world.

In myths, our earliest recorded history, trees have been given magical and religious properties. The best known of these are the myths about the Tree of Life and the Tree of Knowledge. One must wonder why trees have played such important roles in our vision of mankind. They have been consistently tied to our very identity, our ability to think and survive. A treatment of the subject is absent from Sir James Frazer's *The Golden Bough* and other scholarly works about myths and symbolism. Not only has the canopy escaped biological scrutiny, but trees, the biological structures to which we owe our very existence, and the myths associated with them are a relatively unexplored academic realm.

That there is such a thing as a giant pea tree may come as a surprise except to those familiar with eastern American hardwood forests that contain stands of locust. These are flowering trees with fine hard wood that is widely used for fence posts. Many varieties of legume are quite common in the planet's tropics. Their success is generally attributed to nitrogen-fixating abilities of the type found in alfalfa and other legumes. Perhaps for these trees it is less difficult to eke out a living from nitrate-poor tropical soils than it is for other species.

Fifty percent of the tall trees at La Selva are legumes. The most common species is *gavilán* (*Pentaclethra macroloba*), whose height seldom exceeds 110 feet. It is a weak tree whose limbs are unsafe to climb, but like its temperate zone counterpart, the locust, its wood is resistant to fungal and insect attack and is often used in construction.

One cannot easily grasp the size of a tree capable of manufacturing tens of thousands of flowers each day. The almendro's trunk was smooth, like a fluted, Grecian column rising limbless above the jungle's roof to support a hemispheric dome of branches and leaves. A large apartment complex could have fit within the crown's tremendous volume.

Some tropical trees produce massive amounts of flowers in an opulent display of color and aroma that can be seen for miles around. Since individuals of the same species may be separated by hundreds of yards or even miles, it is thought that these flowers act as "billboards" to help pollinators locate familiar sources of pollen and nectar within the confusing array of hundreds of tree species that make up a jungle community. Each day those beacons must be replenished in a seemingly wasteful act of nature because most canopy flowers survive for only twenty-four hours. This results in a carpet of fallen flowers on the forest floor.

Almendro is an excellent example of the type of species that cannot be climbed with standard techniques. Even utility-pole foot spikes and a support belt would have been ineffective. The belt could not girdle the tree's circumference, which was greater than twenty feet, and the dense wood could not be penetrated by spikes, even those driven by the powerful legs of a lumberjack.

Two other methods that have occasionally been used for scaling trees would also have proved fruitless. One was described by Eugene Murray-Aaron in his 1903 book, *The Butterfly Hunters in the Caribbees*. This is the earliest complete description of any kind of tropical tree climbing that I have found in print. Murray-Aaron was the curator and secretary of the American Entomological Society, a post that took him to the tropics on many insect-collecting trips. Sharpened bamboo rungs were driven into a trunk and lengths of bamboo lashed across them, making a ladder. Successive sections of this ladder were fabricated right on the trunk and the climb was limited only by the height of the tree. This is the way the Dyaks of Borneo have climbed large trees for centuries.

A more recent method was used by a team from Oregon State University, under the supervision of William Denison, to climb Oregon's tall Douglas firs. Piton-like lag bolts were driven into the trunks, which were climbed like rock faces. Unfortunately, lag bolts and foot spikes injure trees and leave them susceptible to infection, so it is best not to use this type of method.

I soon learned how frustrating trying to place a rope in a tree can be. I shot an arrow through the screen of leaves and it went over several high limbs. This gave some assurance that if the upper limb broke while I was climbing, I would fall only a few feet before being caught by the next lower branch. The next step, which was to re-place the fishing line with a strong cord, went smoothly at first but soon the line began to bind. After an hour of delicately tugging the light-duty fishing line, the cord finally inched over the limb. The cord bound much worse than the line because it had to lift the weight of the rope. The rope rose with torturous slowness, and in the end two hours' work was lost when the cord broke under the strain. The rope fell, piling up like wet spaghetti, and I was surprised by the force with which the trailing end struck the ground.

I aimed the next shot over a different limb hoping for better luck, but the arrow ricocheted from a branch and became perma-nently tangled in leaves. I broke the line angrily and was beginning to feel that perhaps the canopy was inaccessible. The feeling am-plified because in ten minutes, after I had prepared another arrow, it, too, missed its mark, though fortunately it did not become tangled.

Sundown was at hand by the time a line was again threaded through the almendro's crown. There was little reason to rejoice since I had not progressed far beyond where I had begun hours earlier. Anxious to make some headway before the day ended, I hur-riedly tied the cord to the line and pulled. It rose quickly and in a few seconds the cord was in the tree, leaving me in an optimistic frame of mind for the more challenging conquest of the canopy the next morning.

Dinner was being prepared by Chico, the multitalented cook of La Selva who has been a friend, poet, actor, philosopher, singer, and musician to many who have spent long and secluded months at La Selva. The San José office for the Organization for Tropical Studies (OTS), the consortium of American and Costa Rican universities that own La Selva, had instructed me to prepare my own food since a course of OTS students was supposedly taxing the kitchen to its limits. Chico, however, did not always approve of other cooks in his kitchen, and to my good fortune a plate of food was waiting for me.

A typical Costa Rican meal consists of arroz, frijoles, and carne, which translates into rice, beans, and beef. Foods are often fried and sometimes drenched in fat, though this is not a serious problem at La Selva.

OTS students turned La Selva into a dynamo of research energy. After dinner everyone congregated in the dining room to discuss their particular work and biological topics pertaining to that great unknown, and I think unknowable, entity we call a jungle. Many theories hit the blackboard about why there were so many species of trees, why the jungle was so complex, just how it got to be that way, and how one could discover the forest's deepest secrets.

I felt uncomfortable with the "learning sessions." There was an uncharted gulf between the esoteric dissertations of the students and their professors and the real world. How could a handful of words and some sketchy drawings on a blackboard in any way duplicate the *Urwald's* awesome expression of life?

I went to bed around nine o'clock but was kept awake by the diesel generator. Loud white noise vibrated the skull as the generator performed its duties of illumination and freezing ice. If there was evil lurking in the forest, it was embodied in that machine and the encroachment of civilization. Foul exhaust fumes arose from its shed, which was adjacent to rest rooms, showers, and laundry.

Ten o'clock was the magic moment when the generator shut down for the night. Numbed ears could then recover to be serenaded by a jungle chorus of katydids, crickets, frogs, owls, and a great many other animals sounding territorial warnings and singing songs of love.

I awoke to clanking pots and talking from the kitchen. Night still gripped the forest, but the eastern horizon's shade of gray announced the beginning of dawn, one of the most active times in the forest. Many diurnal animals were awakening and leaving their homes in a race to the day's new blossoms and ripening foods, while nocturnal animals quickly finished their secretive work ahead of the light that could expose their activities.

Normally I would sleep soundly during the early morning, but the anticipation of coming events charged me to alertness. I planned to determine which visitors pollinated the almendro and prepared myself to stay in the canopy continuously for twenty-four hours. A military jungle hammock strung between limbs would be my shelter. I quickly dressed, ate, and headed for the trail. Day was unheralded in the forest and I used my headlamp to follow the path, knowing it was the correct one, yet finding it unfamiliar. The landmarks of the previous day were hidden and the canopy was a uniform black interrupted by ever-brightening patches of sky.

Bats still plied the air for bedtime snacks and many other animals could be seen near the trail; amblypygids, crickets, and spiders were on nearby trunks. A large spider dangled at head height over the trail; its lifeline continued straight up for a hundred feet to an origin lost amid the dark tangle of canopy vegetation. The spider's legs, of a several inch spread, seemed poised to catch flying prey. I stepped closer and the animal quivered, then began winding the silken rope onto its legs, reeling itself up to the distant shadows.

I marveled at the thin line that held the spider's relatively heavy weight and could be eaten for storage, disassembled into its constituent proteins, and recycled indefinitely when other ropes were needed. My ropes were bulky, fragile, and designed to be thrown away once they have been used to stop a fall. Spiders were nature's first rope users—for both climbing and tying things together—and I wondered if the idea of rope was conceived by a primitive naturalist who then put his observations to the test.

Except for biting flies and ants, spiders are the most frequently encountered animals in the jungle. Their role is similar to that of baleen whales. With fine-mesh webs they sieve the jungle's currents for airborne "plankton." Small and large insects, and even lizards, may become ensnared. Once I saw two entrancing, tiny lights spinning like a Fourth of July pinwheel. I thought that perhaps two bioluminescent insects were involved in a mating dance, except that the green beams were continuously glowing. Constant light emission is not characteristic of insects, though certain ground fungi look like radiant clouds in the pitch darkness of basement nights.

The rotating lights, short-circuited batteries of luciferin and luciferace, were silent screams of death. A contented spider was spinning a translucent tomb of silk around a click beetle that had two organs for producing cool biological light. The silk was not to restrain already silenced legs; it was a bag to keep flies and maggots off the precious meal.

High in a treetop some leaves rustled as the shining "cat" eyes of a kinkajou, or honey bear, retreated into dense foliage. Kinkajous are members of the family Procyonidae, the raccoon and coati family. They spend nearly their entire lives in trees and are adept at climbing, primate-like, foot over foot straight up a dangling vine. They even have prehensile tails like new-world monkeys.

The diet of honey bears consists largely of fruits, though they are believed to feed upon insects and small animals as well. Dozens of bromeliad leaves were scattered on the ground below the spot where the kinkajou had been feeding; the ends were nibbled in the way a farmer might chew a sprig of grass. That was possibly new information on their diet. Even now little is known about the habits of these unusual animals. I hoped that a kinkajou would be living in a tree hole near the almendro.

On the Near Loop Trail I heard a very loud "WAAA WAAA WAAA" that echoed plaintively through the trees. The screams moved above the forest and came from what I thought to be a large bird. They were ghostly sounds that could have made an inexperienced hiker decide to return to the station. At the time, that animal was one of the canopy's best-kept secrets and years would pass before my work revealed the bird's true identity.

I looked for the bird until the almendro appeared, a dark sentinel standing far above surrounding trees. My pulse quickened as I stepped off the trail into the dark envelope of ominous vegetation and began groping through resistant vines and waist-high herbs. Damp plant fingers touched my neck and I slapped at them, thinking they were cold-blooded denizens of the basement.

When I was at the tree, pulling the rope into the crown proved easy, but because the almendro was so tall, a standard 165-foot length was too short to reach over its limbs. By the time I discovered this, the free end had already been pulled fifteen feet off the ground, practically out of reach except that a small climbable tree stood nearby. Its branches were stressed by my weight, and the crown swayed off center as the tree threatened to break.

Another climber in this tree was an inch-long paraponera ant.

Paraponera have a powerful sting that has earned them the common name of "bullet ant." Their bodies are built like insect-world tanks, with hard, thick exoskeletons that can ward off the attacks of strong-beaked birds and ignorant arboreal lizards and snakes.

Paraponera are very common and one of the few animals that nest in the ground and forage in the highest trees. Unlike numerous other ant species, they don't nest in trees, even though the canopy is the source of much of their food. They are aggressive hunters and will dismantle wasp nests and attack even larger organisms. They also feed on plant nectar and a variety of insects. I remember seeing a katydid, approximately three inches in length, fall from the canopy onto the trail in front of me with a paraponera clinging to its back.

These ants are unusual in another way. Like crickets, grasshoppers, and cicadas, they have joined the select group of organisms that are capable of producing sound. Their sound is not intended for amorous encounters; rather it is a rasping buzz that is produced when the ant is very agitated. I poked at the paraponera with a twig and it spun around emitting warning screeches, large jaws agape, and not at all concerned that a monster tens of thousands of times its size was inches away. I did not doubt that these ants could challenge any animal large or small.

There is one foe the paraponera cannot fight: the microscopic spores of a group of predatory fungi. Known as entomogenic fungus, its insidious life cycle begins when a spore lands on the exoskeleton of its living prey, virtually any large insect, spider, or related creature. The spore begins growing into a long filamentous hypha that "hunts" for a weak spot in the ant's exoskeleton and passes into the animal's interior. Hyphae proliferate quickly without killing their host until they have entered the reproductive stage.

Mycologists, fungus experts, have noted that most carcasses attacked by predatory fungi are found a few feet above the ground. They suggest that the hyphae can selectively attack an animal's nervous system, causing it to go berserk and climb a small plant where spores of the fungi can be readily dispersed by air currents. The implications of this interaction are enormous. Since the hyphae might use chemical cues to locate the appropriate nerve ganglia and neurons, this would seem a potentially rewarding subject for neurological

64

LIFE ABOVE
THE
JUNGLE
FLOOR

research; predatory fungi might hold a key to a deeper understanding of our own mental processes. These fungi could also serve a more immediate purpose. They are candidates for the biological control of agricultural pests; it is thought that spores might be effective in spray form.

I have found many of these victims eerily "frozen" in their last act of life, some still poised for battle with their invisible enemy, others apparently stopped in stride. Soon after the victim's death the fungi's reproductive tissue emerges from the corpse to form antler-like appendages or thick paintlike coatings that mask the animal's features. At this stage spores are again ready to be released to continue this bizarre life cycle. Fortunately there are no fungi of a similar type that attack mammalian prey.

I grabbed my rope, took it back to the ground, tied it to a second rope, and pulled both into the almendro. I then secured one end of the rope to a tree, slipped on my harness, and began the ascent.

The forest looks incomparably different from above. Three-fourths of the jungle is an aerial habitat, and only climbers or fliers can see it as it really is. During the first twenty feet the ground quickly receded in importance. Climbing caused a feeling that was similar to being harnessed in a hang glider; it was like *being* a flying animal.

The forest's tiers unfolded, level by level, as a kaleidoscope of leaves and plants; each region revealed new assemblages that were at once the same and very different. I rose into the bell-shaped crown of a thirty-foot tree and emerged through its bubble of leaves into a new dimension. I had crossed the arbitrary boundary of the lower canopy.

Numerous smaller trees adapted to the lower zone did not grow above this height. Nor did the ravenous mosquitoes of the ground rise to this level. Perhaps they were reluctant to pass through the lower leaves, but it was more likely that each mosquito species (there are dozens in a tropical forest) had a different set of environmental limits.

Marston Bates has elaborated on mosquito behavior in his book *The Forest and the Sea* in a way that clearly shows how forest insect life is found in layers and how these layers can change depending on the time of day.

In the course of our mosquito studies [in Colombia] we had found that each different species had its characteristic flight habits. Some kinds were found only near the ground, others only high in the trees; some that were most common high in the trees in the morning or afternoon would come down near the ground during the midday hours, showing a sort of daily vertical migration.

While I was explaining this to my friend, it struck me that this is just the way animals act in the sea. Most life is near the top, because that is where the sunlight strikes and everything below depends on this surface. Life in both the forest and the sea is distributed in horizontal layers.

Bates compared the forest floor to the ocean's bottom, or benthos, where plankton and other pelagic organisms eventually fall to rest. Like the benthos, the forest's ground zone is a garbage dump. And the garbage, be it decaying wood, leaves, fruit, or flowers, is rich in energy—energy that can support odd snakelike amphibians known as caecilians, numerous frogs, agoutis, pacas, deer, tapirs, rabbits, and a variety of other organisms. In a crude biological sense, these ground animals are scavengers that live off manna from the jungle's heaven. They in turn feed ground predators like the large cats, mink-like tayras, and poisonous snakes such as the coral, fer-de-lance, and bushmaster.

If the ground level is the forest's benthos, it is also the forest's "basement." Basements have unvarying humidity and temperature, low light levels, and musty air that would seem to need circulation. The forest basement is a gloomy and depressing zone that over the centuries has given birth to numerous oppressive stories of exploration. These stories have resulted in an incorrect view of the jungle because they come from a zone that only represents about a third of the community. Above the forest's basement is its "main level" where most forest activity takes place. Each of the higher levels has a different microclimate determined by increasing extremes in light levels, humidity, wind, and temperature. These microclimates profoundly affect the forest's organisms.

The tiers of the main level are populated by a mixed assortment of animals. Some are equally at home in the basement and treetops, while others live an exclusively arboreal life. For example, anteaters, coatis, and boas move freely between the ground and the upper levels in search of food. Monkeys, sloths, kinkajous, and vast numbers of organisms from insects through vertebrates spend nearly their entire lives high in the aerial jungle. As research accumulates we are finding that species once considered rare at ground level are actually quite common up in the canopy.

At thirty feet I was above the point that could be reached by basement-bound scientists who used collecting poles and portable ladders. This was the arbitrary boundary of the unexplored lower canopy. Wisps of wind hinted that the upper canopy would be a fresher environment. The basement's perpetual high humidity and near constant 80 degree temperatures had been uncomfortable. Although the temperature had not changed perceptibly, I knew the blazing heat of the tropical sun waited above. Even so, I would be much cooler in the upper canopy because the heat would be blunted by evaporative cooling in the low-humidity air.

The trees of the lower canopy are lucky individuals that somehow survived the basement's onslaught of leaf and seed eaters, not to mention falling trees and limbs. Unless a gap opens to let in light for growth, many established but small trees succumb to old age and/or disease before they become reproductively mature. So active are the forces destroying seed and seedlings that possibly less than one in ten million reach this zone. By the time a tree grows into the upper canopy and full sunlight, perhaps fifty million or more of its siblings have died.

With an increase in height, a canopy mirage appeared. The tops of small tree crowns fused into an undulating mat of green producing a "false floor" that gave me a deceptive feeling of comfort. Flowers that had not been visible from the ground dotted tree crowns and attracted visitors such as butterflies, wasps, and beetles. The showiest tree, *Warscewiczia coccinea*, sported tassels of scarlet leaves that advertised the presence of minute, orange, nectar-producing flowers. Its red necklaces looked much like poinsettia and occasionally attracted snowcap hummingbirds.

Hummingbirds have acquired an almost mythical aura as pollinators of jungle plants. If they are seen at flowers, such as warscewiczia, it is often assumed that they must be pollinating the plant. But hummingbirds are not munificent pollinators. They are tainted by self-serving motives, as are all forms of life, and would just as soon steal nectar without reimbursing the plant by carrying pollen to distant flowers.

All species of flowers have learned about the self-indulgent attitudes of pollinators the hard way. Ages of evolution have given many angiosperm families convoluted and often intricately shaped flower parts, such as are common in orchids and legumes. These intricate structures force potential thieves to contact pollen when they visit a flower.

Reproductive success is an outgrowth of a flower's shape and color, which must conform to the structure and behavior of particular animals. This often gives the strongest clues as to which of a plant's many visitors are the actual pollinators. Although flowers pollinated by hummingbirds can have a variety of forms, they typically are red, produce large quantities of nectar, and are trumpet-shaped to match the beak length of a particular bird. Warscewiczia has only one of these features: red leaves. It is a fact, however, that red is attractive to more than birds; butterflies seem especially interested in red and orange.

More important is that warscewiczia flowers, though they have long been considered to be pollinated by hummingbirds, have no contrivance that would force hummingbirds to be anything but robbers. The flowers are small and rather unspecialized, typical characteristics of a large number of tropical rain forest trees and smaller plants that are routinely pollinated by a variety of insects. My aerial observations over many years suggest that the pollination of this tree is far more likely due to butterflies, beetles, and wasps that frequent its flowers than to hummingbirds.

At a level of about fifty feet I had left below many unpleasantries of the basement; however, a growing fear of height took their place. We humans are different from arboreal primates in that recently, in an evolutionary sense, we have acquired an accentuated fear of heights. The fact that man's ancestors were arboreal can be seen in our various body parts. Fingers, for example, were originally designed for grasping limbs, and an opposable thumb made that grip even more effective. Though the hand has been somewhat modified over the millennia, it remains for all practical purposes an organ for climbing and grasping.

When we look at the foot, however, a different story unfolds. Our ancestors had grasping feet that looked like hands. The remnants of this ancient refinement are our shriveled toes; the "palms" have been deformed by the heavy burden of walking upright. We are clubfooted apes lacking very important locomotor devices for clambering safely in tall trees. Is it so surprising, then, that we have a healthy respect for heights?

Add to our crippled status the fact that we are very large and climbing becomes an activity fraught with danger. Except for larger arboreal mammals such as sloths and orangutans, denizens of the canopy weigh no more than a few pounds. In fact, most are much smaller than that. The prevalence of small climbers is in part due to a physical principle best illustrated by another example.

Consider a mouse and a man that have fallen from a tall tree. When the mouse hits the ground it will probably become disoriented but no serious injuries will result, whereas the fall could be fatal for the large-bodied man. In proportion to its weight a mouse has relatively more surface area, which allows air friction to effectively slow its fall. One might expect that large animals should be no worse off: as body size increases so does surface area. The problem is that body weight increases more rapidly than surface area, and above approximately ten pounds, arboreal existence becomes an increasingly deadly game of chance.

Body weight has another drawback worth mentioning. Consider again the falling mouse and a 175-pound man. The mouse will likely pass a branch that it could catch to stop its descent. The situation for the man is considerably more difficult. His stored potential energy one hundred feet above the ground is 17,500 foot-pounds. After falling only five feet this man's kinetic energy (energy of motion) would translate into his body weight multiplied by five. The effort needed to stop would be comparable to the man desperately trying to hold on to a large limb with four of his equally heavy companions clinging to him.

What happens if the man falls fifteen feet and "luckily" hits a limb square in his midsection? The force delivered to the limb is 2,635 foot-pounds. If the limb were the right size, it would bend, absorbing the shock and reducing the possibility of injury, but the largest percentage of tree limbs would keep on bending and the man would fall past. An improbable succession of the right-sized limbs would be necessary in order for him to arrive at the ground safely. This should adequately dispel any ideas about the possibility of jumping from a burning high-rise building and surviving; the fireman's safety net is useful only for falls from moderate heights.

A peculiar aspect of treetop animal life is that many inhabitants belong to groups that in other parts of the world are found living under stones and fallen trees, in fields, dirt, and sand. These include rare and odd species of spiders, scorpions, centipedes, lizards, frogs, and other organisms we have come to associate with the ground. Largely a terrestrial community, they were "elevated" into the trees at some time in the distant past and have since evolved into a more or less distinct community.

A look at the vertical distribution of cockroaches (from my collection of 40,000 specimens in 200 insect families) will give insight into some evolutionary forces, in addition to gravity, that have shaped canopy organisms. The ground has a profusion of large-bodied, darkly pigmented species that feed on a variety of foods that drop from the canopy. Dark coloration is a camouflage that matches the world of decaying and composting debris. The fallen material also forms complexes of random hiding places that are many different sizes and shapes.

Foods are abundant in the canopy, yet there are relatively fewer hiding places to be found on the thin branches where leaf litter cannot accumulate. The large, ground-zone type cockroaches have given way to smaller, aerial varieties endowed with unexpected beauty. Translucent shields, tinted green or tan, camouflage these aerial roaches when they are sitting exposed on leaves and their diminutive size is suited to hiding in the crease of a leaf or by a small bit of moss. They are more likely to be overlooked by canopy birds that treasure roaches as food. Bigger limbs do collect epiphytes and decaying debris and that is where large, dark, basementlike cockroaches can most likely be found.

Another interesting group of canopy cockroaches fly by day, and the inexperienced eye can easily mistake them for certain beetles. One of these, *Paratropes bilunata*, has a very conspicuous color pattern of yellow, black, and brown, which mimics a lycid beetle. The deception extends beyond coloration since the roach also flies and behaves like a beetle. My observations show that paratropes visit flowers and may pollinate certain treetop plants such as *Oreopanax*, an arboreal bush. No other cockroach has aspired to a higher status in the eyes of mankind.

Not all canopy organisms have been similarly modified into sensational forms. The treetops are much like a treasure chest. Within their unexplored reaches, on branches invisible from the ground and too weak to climb, there are uncounted jewels still to be described, and many, no doubt, could prove extremely useful to mankind.

I left the lower canopy at an arbitrary boundary of around sixty-five feet and entered the upper canopy. I sat there quietly watching for animal activities but noticed only the silence. There were no calling birds, and the small manakins, black-and-white birds of the basement, had ceased snapping their wings as part of their courtship rituals. Howler monkeys were not to be heard. It was long past their usual sunrise screaming sessions when troop warned troop to stay away from their respective territories. And the mind-penetrating buzz of cicadas was thankfully gone. The forest is often silent.

One ominous sound punctuated the silence: it was the sound of overburdened limbs, clumps of epiphytes, and large fruits and seeds intermittently crashing to the ground. The forest is always growing and reaching, suicidally in some cases, for the sun. The jungle's vast sea of weak trees and rapidly growing epiphytes are plant-world Icaruses destined to fall. Limbs become weak from rapid growth, resulting in fungal attack, while epiphytes become heavy and/or loose their grip. The background noise was worrisome and I wondered if the additional 175 pounds would cause my limb to fall.

During wind storms one is certain to hear the booming crash of toppling trees or actually be able to watch them fall. Dendrologists, or tree experts, have found that the turnover rate of forest, the average time it takes for an acre of forest to fall and be replaced, is about 110 years at La Selva. Many trees live much longer than that, perhaps several hundred years, while others live less than a dozen.

"Fallout" adds an element of risk to jungle walks, and on windy days trees that have large seed pods should be avoided. It is not uncommon for jungle trees to have weighty seeds and fruit for a variety of reasons, one being that for seedlings to survive in the shady, low-energy, forest basement, they may need ample food reserves to become established.

The Brazil nut tree, *Bertholletia excelsa*, which produces the nut of the same name, exemplifies the fatal potential of falling objects. These trees grow exclusively in the wild and attain heights that can exceed 150 feet. Fifteen to thirty nuts are packed in an extremely hard pod that is four to six inches in diameter. The combined weight of nut and pod can be up to five pounds, and since the pods develop in the tree's crown, which is one hundred feet up, they hit the ground with tremendous force. Edwin A. Menninger, in his book *Edible Nuts of the World*, recounts that the pods are "exceedingly dangerous missiles. Every year there are reports of Castanhieros [the name given to the Indians or migrant laborers who gather the nuts] killed or badly injured by falling fruits [pods]. Mostly the gatherers stay clear of the trees when it is raining or windy, but occasionally they work carrying a round wooden shield over their heads to ward off the falling pods. The entire Brazil nut industry, set in the suffocating tropical forest of the Amazon, with itinerant gatherers bartering their nuts to jungle traders operating from wheezy boats or tiny trading factories, is in startling and delightful contrast to the mechanized, scientific agriculture we know."

Brazil nut trees are not found at La Selva, but the monkey pot tree, *Lecythis ampla*, is. Both trees belong to the same family, Lecythidaceae, a family also known for its large seed pods and tasty nuts. Only the Brazil nut has been harvestable in quantities large enough to make them a commercial success even though, according to Menninger, the monkey pot tree has nuts of "delicate flavor and considered by some to be the finest nut known."

Unlike Brazil nuts, sapucaia nuts, the name of those from the monkey pot tree, are usually taken by canopy animals. Though rare at La Selva, monkey pot trees make fascinating landmarks because the dozens of pods strewn below a tree look like cast-away urns of an ancient culture. Monkey pot trees equal the size of Brazil nut trees with the added feature that pods can exceed the size of a bowling ball and weigh up to ten pounds. The noise and vibration caused by one of these pods striking the ground could inspire awe even in a Stoic.

At first I found the rock and sway of climbing unsettling, since I was still very much a ground-loving primate. And entrusting my life to a climbing rope whose diameter was equal to the width of my little finger seemed less than sensible. Even though the rope had a 2,000-pound breaking strength, any number of incidents would quickly reduce its strength. I began having terrifying thoughts that now seem ridiculous. I imagined that my rope could have been gnawed nearly in two by a variety of animals that would be attracted to the salt lost from sweaty hands, or that a monkey in a flash of insight would sever the rope to keep invaders out of his canopy home, or that a knot would simply come undone. Being in no position to check these possibilities, they became greatly magnified.

After an hour, the first limb of the almendro loomed overhead and I found myself climbing with increasing speed toward this "stable ground." Panting and sweaty, I arrived at a limb that was a yard in diameter. It was a relief to be there, and after only a moment's inspection I sat down in the middle of a fantastic garden of large-leaved plants, orchids, anthuriums, and bromeliads whose arrangement seemed as "thought out" as a Zen garden.

Yet something was amiss here. A peculiar pattering noise came from leaves near the seat of my pants. Ants were milling about, as ants do when they are mad, because I was squashing their home. They were vigorously snapping their unique, spring-loaded jaws against the leaves. These rudimentary acoustics were not as highly evolved as that of the paraponera, but the message was the same, so I jumped up and made my way along the limb.

The limb was covered with a thick layer of moss: a fine, natural shag carpet that ended at an upright branch equal to my waist in girth. I edged along the carpet, passing many varieties of plants that I did not recognize, and sat in an inviting patch of moss to lean against the upright limb. It was as comfortable as an easy chair and I savored the joy of finally having arrived at an upper canopy community.

This was a wilderness never seen by mankind. It was devoid of human progress, its cigarette butts, bottle caps, and other ejecta. On the whole planet, from the oceans to the highest peaks, there was no more pristine a setting. No photograph can capture the beauty of this bewildering place: the fleeting impressions and smells, the chasms of cascading leaves, and islands of ornamental plants awash in the airy sea.

The aerial gardens were vaguely reminiscent of cliffs and rock ledges in the Sierra Nevadas that support varieties of wild flowers, bushes, and conifers. Over thousands of years bare rocks are able to collect enough drifting soil particles for plants to take root. Trees of the tropics are short-lived in comparison, and it seems unlikely that communities of life would establish themselves on curved limb surfaces, especially to those of us who live in northern temperate regions. Our trees bear only mosses, lichens, fungi, algae, and ferns and generally these are not too numerous, with the Olympic Peninsula of Washington State being an exception. Spanish moss is one epiphyte that has found its way into the southern United States. It is not really a moss but a "colony" of tiny bromeliads linked into long, pendulous chains.

Early explorers were so unaccustomed to epiphytes that they did not recognize them as separate entities. Christopher Columbus may have been the first person to comment upon the peculiar look of epiphytes that adorn tree limbs, although he mistook them as being parts of the supporting tree. Eugene Murray-Aaron writes in *The Butterfly Hunters:*

> . . . many of them . . . had branches of many kinds, although growing from one trunk; and one branch is of one kind and another of another kind, and so different that the diversity of the kinds is the greatest wonder of the world; for instance, one branch had leaves like those of cane, and another like those of mastic; and thus on a single tree were five or six of these kinds.

One should not judge Columbus's error too harshly for his was a time when geese hatched from goose barnacles, mud gave birth to frogs, flies were born from feces, and monsters populated distant lands. To suggest that a tree was made of several different species was one of the more believable claims of that time. Interestingly enough, a similar mistake is occasionally made today because epiphytes can be so populous it is difficult to distinguish which leaves belong to the host tree.

William Beebe, a renowned explorer at the beginning of this

century, was the first to clearly state the importance of jungle tree-tops as a major center for the planet's life:

> The mid-jungle was the heart of the tropical life. Here I could no longer feel myself on equal terms in height. I had most painfully to crane my neck upward, and to study the inhabitants of this suspended cosmos with glasses or shotgun. Here . . . the great pigeons, the motmots, jacamars, trogons . . . sang, fed, courted and nested . . . the big tree-frogs boomed, and the sloths vegetated from birth until the claws of a harpy eagle gripped them. Orchids, air-plants and lianas rioted, and unknown growths dropped a myriad of plummets, a warp of aerial roots; threads until they reached the ground, then becoming in turn twine, cord, rope and cable. It was the great center of life of the South American jungles, a zone vibrating with myriad forms suspended half-way between heaven and earth. . . .

When seeing a jungle one may wonder what it is about the tropics that makes certain land areas so rich with treetop life. If we were to mull over the possibilities, two features emerge that are essential. All lush canopy communities are found in warm climates and all have a nearly constant rainy season and/or heavy fog. Even in tropical forests that receive as much as twelve feet of rain per year, aerial communities will be absent if the jungle has a substantial dry season. La Selva does not have a severe dry season and its climate has nurtured one of the earth's finest canopy communities. Besides lowland rain forests, tropical cloud forests on windward mountain slopes also have well-developed canopy communities. Clouds formed by rising humid air lose their moisture as fine rain and dripping fog.

Probably the most serious threat to certain canopy communities is the climatic effect of deforestation. In the Amazon Basin, for example, up to three-fourths of the annual precipitation comes from moisture released into the air by foliage. If enough trees are removed, the precipitation cycle will be broken, and the result will be extended dry periods that will decimate canopy communities and all vegetation having high moisture requirements.

Most epiphytes are not like ordinary plants; they seem capable of surviving on limbs devoid of any apparent nutrient or water supplies. The hardiest epiphytes are the so-called atmospheric epiphytes, or air plants. Their nutrients come from minute amounts of dust dissolved in rain along with scant material that is leached by rain from bark surfaces. Some common groups of air plants include lichens, bromeliads, and orchids. Air plants are the first to colonize bare limbs and the hardiest of them are found high in a tree's crown, the hottest and driest of canopy locations. It is essential that these plants be able to obtain water from humid air.

Aerial plants, such as certain bromeliads, have stumbled upon an extraordinary manner for obtaining water and nutrients. Their leaf bases overlap, forming tight bowls. The long, curved leaves spread in a large radius around the plant and act as gutters to collect rain, filling their private reservoirs.

Next to me on the almendro limb was one of the forest's largest bromeliads. Its leaves covered a diameter of six feet and were edged with sharp thorns. I carefully pulled at a leaf to examine the cistern and startled some of the occupants. A brown katydid three inches in length aimlessly rebounded between the leaves; its powerful hind jumping legs were ineffective on the glassy surfaces. The katydid was followed by others of its kind, and for a minute the bromeliad was the site of much chaotic hopping before all had found freedom, all except one, which I collected.

The katydid's forewings were the color of dried leaves, a common camouflage, with a matching set of attractive black designs that mimicked a dead portion of leaf. It was a stocky creature, or in the language of an entomologist, robust. Later I misplaced the specimen at the Los Angeles County Museum of Natural History. I searched through their large collection hoping to find it and discovered that there were no others resembling the one that had been lost. To this day I wonder if the katydid with the picture wings was an unknown species.

Katydids are not the only inhabitants that can be found in the tanks of bromeliads. The largest animals are frogs and their tadpoles, which subsist on smaller organisms such as mosquito larvae, fly larvae, beetle larvae, algae, and microorganisms. Dragonflies deposit their eggs in bromeliad ponds. In drier areas one can find a variety of beetle larvae, spiders, sow bugs, cockroach eggs and adults, pseudoscorpions, and even earthworms. A side benefit for the bromeliad is that animals bring in nutrients both in their feces and when they die. Bromeliads have an effective means of absorbing these nutrients through special leaf pores that are absent in other plants.

It may seem puzzling that the bromeliad would need to protect itself with thorns, but perhaps the thorns originated as a defense against grazing kinkajous or became necessary to guard the thriving communities from a variety of canopy insectivores; after all, it would do a bromeliad little good to have animals ransacking its leaves and digging into its tank to reach the delicious residents. There is another possible reason for the evolution of thorns. Large bromeliads hold up to a gallon of water—precious water needed to survive through dry spells—and thorns would possibly ward off thirsty arboreal mammals and birds.

Water-impounding bromeliads are one of the most successful of New World epiphytes, capable of forming dense impenetrable colonies that in effect are treetop swamps. This much water is heavy and it is possible that a group of bromeliads can lead to breaking limbs, but it seems extremely unlikely that they would contribute significantly to the large number of tree falls that occur at La Selva.

At first glance the epiphytes that decorated the almendro limbs reminded me of desert plants. They had tough, succulent stems and leaves, and thick tissues are ideal for storing water. Cacti have been able to invade the canopy environment because they possess these adaptations.

The similarity between canopy and desert plants is superficial. Jungle limbs can be as dry as desert soil between rainstorms, but unlike desert air, canopy air is a virtual ocean of moisture from which canopy plants can directly obtain water. On cool mornings fogs and mists are commonplace and epiphytes easily absorb this moisture through leaf stomata; in addition, dew drips into root mats and humus that cover many limb surfaces. Epiphytes are exotic weaklings—hothouse varieties—that depend on the earth's wettest climates for their survival. Remove them from a warm, humid environment, place them in the low humidity of a real desert, and they will quickly perish.

The prospect of returning to the rope and stepping into space was intimidating and my mind rehearsed the potential hazards; this was something I would often do during the first years of canopy work. When I finally did step from the almendro limb, I immediately began falling, as if the rope had broken. I grabbed at the limb, digging into the moss with my fingers on the way down. After falling a couple of feet, I jerked to a stop—the rope had only been stretching and lowering me until it became taut.

The tree crown, which was fully within the forest's upper canopy zone, had its own strata of communities: low, sizable branches had more extensive populations of large epiphytes while each higher, smaller limb had fewer epiphytes, and these were of different species. Smaller limbs held less moisture and were generally closer to the forest's upper surface, thus on a smaller scale, the inside of a large tree crown possesses microclimatic gradients similar to the forest as a whole.

Many epiphytes depend primarily upon wind and birds to disperse their seeds. Relying on wind for dispersal generally necessitates the production of many small seeds, as in the case of ferns and mosses, which have numerous spores for riding the gentlest air currents to new growth sites. Orchids, one of the more common epiphytes, also have microscopic seeds, up to 3.5 million per plant in some species, while other plants, some bromeliads among them, have dandelion-like "parachutes" for floating larger seeds to distant limbs. Because microscopic seeds are so small and contain few nutrients to help a seedling compete with other plants, they generally must land on a smooth surface to become established. The forest air is literally full of these "propagules" and all surfaces are sprinkled by this living dust. Equipment and ropes left exposed to the elements, like boats left moored in the ocean, become covered with a layer of life in just a few months.

Dispersal by birds could help to account for some of the great differences of epiphyte community size between tree crowns. Some trees, like the monkey pot and silk cotton, are overendowed with epiphytes, while others are barren. Unlike wind dispersal, dispersal by birds is not a random process. Canopy birds follow more or less consistent foraging routes that include trees which already contain mature epiphytes along with their fruits and delectable inhabitants. Trees that are unattractive to birds, unless they fall under or along these routes, are colonized much more slowly.

Epiphytes benefit the forest by significantly adding to a forest's vital store of organic material. These nutrients eventually find their way into all jungle trees. One would think that rain would have to wash treetop nutrients to the ground before a tree could benefit from them; that is if a tree's roots are found only in the ground. This is an area in which scientists are making some truly startling discoveries. Nalini Nadkarni, of the University of California at Santa Barbara, has found that some trees do not conform to common logic. True they do have roots in the ground, but very surprisingly they also have "crown roots" growing from their limbs. Crown roots do not plunge groundward in search of the earth's soil as aerial roots would; rather they grow along the limbs in search of arboreal soil. This soil comes from debris that collects and decomposes in the mats of epiphyte roots, which can be many inches thick. In effect, epiphytes pay "rent" for limb space in the form of nutrients, a commodity in short supply throughout the forest.

At about one hundred feet, the height equal to a ten-story building, full sunlight, distant treetops, and flitting butterflies burst into view. At that point the upper canopy was left below and I had risen into the forest's highest zone, the emergent layer, comprised almost solely of immense crowns of giant trees that have grown much taller than the surrounding forest. From within the almendro's airy spaces birds could be seen hundreds of yards away. The sun, merely a distant star from the vantage of the basement, scorched the upper surface with brilliant light, and tropical birds emblazoned the forest with fleeting glimpses of rainbow hues. This was the exclusive world of skilled arboreal animals.

The sparsely populated almendro crown was decorated by pastel orange blossoms of a hardy atmospheric orchid as well as tens of thousands of its own flowers. The air was redolent with a heady fragrance. Beyond the crown, treetops crowded one another like various-sized cabbage heads of a garden gone wild. The stunning pink of almendro flowers dotted the vast, undulating forest roof all the way to the Cordillera Central, the mountainous spine of Central America. Vulcans Barba and Poas rose majestically from those peaks, cloaked by the jungle's green.

Near my destination, at 140 feet, I began to feel an odd sensation that became stronger with each moment. Although I was a foreigner in the canopy, I had a clear memory of having been there before, which was very puzzling. Though there are many possible explanations, I wonder if our brains' circuitry might retain vestigial nerve tracks along with the associations between visual and other centers of perception that were designed specifically to interpret arboreal environments. Perhaps these vestigial circuits were stimulated, and it was they that gave rise to my sense of *déjà vu*. It has been mentioned that many of our organs retain an arboreal heritage both in function and appearance: hands and thumbs were designed for climbing, gripping branches, snatching insects, and collecting food; elongated limbs were for locomotion and feeding in a three-dimensional space where support surfaces for movement were not only underfoot but overhead and at the sides; stereoscopic color vision gave a very accurate system for locating food and judging movement along weak limbs, and an enlarged brain provided the "computing equipment" needed to exist in a very complicated aerial environment. This was the basis of human intelligence. Why then shouldn't our brains' processes retain some functioning elements of their past?

I climbed onto a stout, narrow limb where I intended to stay many hours. Sitting on a small limb is about as comfortable as sitting on a two-by-four, so I was pleased to see that the limb's configuration would support my hammock. The hammock was made of lightweight rip-stop nylon and designed like a tent for inclement weather. Hanging the hammock proved difficult and frightening. I crawled out onto the limb and it began swaying, threatening to throw me off. A slip would have sent me swinging from my safety line with bruising force against the trunk. It took an hour to connect the lines that held up the hammock's tent, and because there were not enough nearby limbs to do this properly, I made a framework of bamboo sticks to support the tent's rain fly. The rain fly was independently secured with strings to nearby branches, which, if everything went well, would hold it like a roof over the hammock and keep me dry. The project was finished by 9 A.M.

This work had been physically and mentally strenuous, so when I lay back in the hammock it was with a mixture of relief and trepidation; I could not stop thinking of the ground 140 feet below.

Throughout the preparatory period I had watched the crown and listened for arriving bees. I continued to do so from the hammock, but the observations were of little consequence as there were only a few bees to be seen. (During an earlier part of the year the crown would have been noisy with the buzz of dozens of species of bees, many of them rare and some unknown.) After hours of watching, listening, and daydreaming, I was finally rewarded with a peculiar sight. It looked as though a small, yellow, radio-controlled aircraft was banking left around a tree crown and coming my way. The craft was in fact a beetle with a pair of motionless bright yellow forewings that had aerodynamic capability and furiously beating hind wings that acted like propellers. I later discovered that this animal was the largest wood-boring buprestid beetle, *Euchroma gigantea*, in the New World.

By noon the weather began to change. Huge cumulonimbus clouds were moving in from the Caribbean seaboard. I considered leaving but could not forsake seeing the pollinators, which possibly would arrive later in the day or even during the night. It was unknown then that canopy bees were rare after the middle of July even if there were ample flowers to attract them. I checked the rain fly and hoped the hammock would live up to my expectations, then relaxed and snacked on a peanut-butter-and-jelly sandwich and fruit juice from my pack.

As the storm drew near, I began to doubt the wisdom of staying in the tree. The arriving cloud was overwhelming. It covered a hundred-square-mile area and skimmed over the lowlands vacuuming up hot air saturated with expired jungle moisture that rose tens of thousands of feet, cooled, and condensed into droplets.

The serenity of the treetops was interrupted by the impending storm, which had begun to swallow the eastern woods in a gray wall of rain. The storm sounded like a huge waterfall as turbulent air began tearing at the forest's roof, violently shaking trees on an adjacent ridge. I braced myself as the front raced to engulf the almendro.

When the gusts hit, the hammock felt like a flag in a stiff breeze. I lay there tense and quite motionless, like a cadaver, except for my eyes, which were busy watching. The tree shuddered and its monolithic trunk, which would have seemed unlikely to bend under any circumstance, leaned with the storm. That was when I took strong notice of a feature that I had tried to ignore: the trunk did not rise straight to the canopy but followed a course plotted when it was a young tree searching for an opening in the roof. It gave the impression of a drunk leaning over its feet, and each time the massive column moved more off center I thought it might uproot.

Delicate limbs, the size of my thigh and smaller, flailed like whips in defiance of the wind's surging currents. There were short moments of relative calm between these assaults, when I was able to gather my senses and appreciate that the tree was still standing. This buffeting was the storm's dry cycle, whose main effect was to shake feeble residents from the trees.

The first gusts seemed endless, but they could not have lasted more than a couple of minutes before being joined by buckets of spray. I had long abandoned any hope of remaining dry and received the rain blowing into the hammock with detached resignation. The situation became markedly more discouraging as a round of savage gusts ripped some stays loose. The rain fly struggled to be aloft like a kite, and a river of rain began flowing off the roof directly into the cot; within a few seconds it held more water than a colony of bromeliads. The reservoir quickly rose above my belly.

Contrary to popular belief, tropical rain is not warm, and my arboreal pond felt like an ice bath. Fearing that accumulating water would break the limb, I stabbed drainage holes in the nylon tarp. These were insufficient to keep up with inflowing water and I did not dare enlarge the holes as that could have ruined the hammock. I climbed onto the limb, dumped the water, and reconnected the lines of the rain fly. Standing directly in the wind increased my chill. My clothing was soaked, I was shivering, my fingers were pale and inflexible. This made work exceedingly difficult and even my thinking became labored.

I sat back in the hammock, in the early stages of hypothermia, watching the water level slowly rise. The inpouring streams could not be stopped and my clothing had no chance of drying before nightfall. The simplest tasks became increasingly difficult and the chance of making a stupid mistake seemed imminent. Reluctantly, I gave up my plans to stay overnight and prepared to descend.

I had only two more days at La Selva before returning to California, not enough time to devise a dry means of camping in the canopy, so further research into the pollination biology of the almendro had to wait another year, but I returned to California satisfied that my tree-climbing techniques would prove very valuable for investigators of treetop communities.

Extinction
of the Dinosaurs

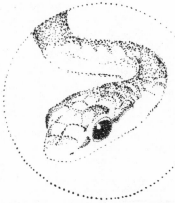

OCEANS, SHORES, rivers, lakes, the ground, and sky are some of the planet's paramount habitats. Within them, inanimate ingredients have directed the evolutionary course of life. The fusiform shape of a fish is dictated by the medium in which it lives, just as soil has determined the shape of moles with bodies for burrowing, and rolling plains have given rise to cursorial, long-legged animals such as deer and horses. A monkey, in contrast, has been formed in the canopy, an environment defined largely by living things: the trunks of trees, limbs, vines, and epiphytes. This habitat stands apart from all others because it, too, just like monkeys, fish, deer, and horses, is a product of evolution.

The history of this species factory is in some ways analogous to the development of manufacturing during the industrial revolution. Early factories were crude affairs that over time and with accumulated knowledge became increasingly sophisticated, resulting in more refined products. Likewise, organic evolution has given the canopy an increasingly complex face that in turn has pushed arboreal inhabitants to new evolutionary frontiers.

A factory contains a bewildering array of tools for fashioning products such as cars or electron microscopes, and without some prior knowledge, a factory's operations can be wholly unfathomable. Such is the situation in the canopy, where all of its products, the trees themselves, parrots, monkeys, and philodendrons are final models whose ancestral links in the canopy's ancient past are mostly a mystery.

In the summer of 1979 I stumbled upon a key part of that mystery in the form of several pecan-sized seeds resting on a muddy trail. They appeared to be the seeds of a plant-world dinosaur, a gymnosperm relict known as *Gnetum* that had somehow survived through a great revolutionary period of the earth's history. The events of this period, the late Cretaceous, have been a continuing subject of biological controversy for more than a century. During that time entire groups of organisms became extinct on a grand scale: the dinosaurs, pterosaurs (or pterodactyls), and ancient gymnosperm forests disappeared from the earth and were replaced by more "advanced" mammals, birds, and flowering plants.

I asked Mike Grayum, an expert botanist of the Missouri Botanical Gardens, to visit the site and make a positive identification of the seeds. Information on *Gnetum*'s natural history might shed some light on the ecological battles that exterminated the dinosaurs. (Several theories for the demise of the dinosaurs will be discussed in later chapters.) After a twenty-minute walk we found the seeds, and without hesitating Mike confirmed that they were from *Gnetum*. *Gnetum* has large, striped seeds that are very distinctive to the eye of a tropical botanist.

Several *Gnetum* vines dangled beside an emergent pea tree, *Hymenolobium pulcherimum*, whose trunk was two yards in diameter. Mike looked through the vines and selected one that was about the thickness of my thigh. It grew uncertainly at first, in great loops that eventually straightened and disappeared through the leaves of a hundred-foot-tall *Pentaclethra* tree, which ended seven stories below the top of the emergent. Here was a gymnosperm like no other. Yews and conifers were the gymnosperms I knew. This was a vine as large as any in the forest.

The lowest limbs of the *Hymenolobium* were 120 to 130 feet above ground and the rope had to be placed higher still, nearly out of range of my crossbow. Nothing seemed unusual on the climb until I rose above the *Pentaclethra* crowns at the upper surface. Normally, emergents would have limbs that joined with shorter trees, but in this case other canopy trees looked like mere bushes at the *Hymenolobium*'s waist. The tree's limbs thrust upward, seemingly without limit, and being suspended from the towering giant elicited deep feelings of adventure and danger such as I have not felt in another tree.

At 120 feet I noticed that my rope's support limb was partially rotten. I continued up the rope, deciding that this would be no more risky than descending. During the next twenty feet my full concentration was given to climbing delicately, carefully listening for the dreaded sound of snapping wood. Once I was on top of the decayed support, the problem was eliminated by stringing the rope over a higher, healthy branch.

I sat on the rotten limb and took in the panorama with a mixture of joy and disgust. In one direction the forest seemed to be abundant and relatively untouched, but in the opposite direction, toward Puerto Viejo, the forest was gone. La Selva was surrounded by clearings on all but one side; pasture was poised to overrun this island of jungle.

Magnificent *Gnetum* vines entwined the *Hymenolobium*'s topmost limbs and I observed them as a doctor might view a distinguished but terminally ill patient. I was part of the plant's problem. Like the vile missionary who takes disease, lies, and tragedy to isolated tribes, I was a human who brought wastes, airplanes, automobiles, houses, roads, pipelines, power lines, sewage, and insidious pollutants to the world. I was the human who eats McDonald's hamburgers, or any burgers whose meat comes from cattle raised in tropical lands. The chance of *Gnetum* being spared seemed improbable.

Gnetum's leaves shook gently in the warm breeze and sun rays danced across several of its red and burgundy "fruits," organs that told an entrancing story of biological revolution, of surviving through one of the earth's great periods of death. *Gnetum* is a botanical enigma lying outside the main line of gymnosperm ancestry. It has traveled through hundreds of millions of years of evolution secretly, leaving no trace of its origins. This journey is all the more mysterious because *Gnetum* has a remarkable feature almost universally absent in other gymnosperms. Fruit encases its seeds, a trait that is in contradiction to the very meaning of gymnosperm, which translated means "naked seed."

Several botanical sources claimed *Gnetum* fruits to be tasty, so I picked one that was dark and ripe and squeezed it until grape-like juice ran from the tissue. It smelled edible but tropical fruit can be poisonous so I tasted it cautiously. The juice was sweet, which immediately convinced me that in ecological, if not botanical, fact *Gnetum* did have fruit. According to Menninger, *Gnetum* nuts are starchy and nutritious, being "very important food of the jungle tribes," and are prepared by boiling or frying.

Gnetum fruits and the tale of how they came to be offer a fascinating story that may help explain what became of the dinosaurs and why today's jungles are what they are. The theory, published in *Science* (1978) by Philip Regal, is not so much about the demise of dinosaurs as about the evolution and explosive radiation of angiosperms, or flowering plants, and how this caused a fundamental change in the dinosaurs' primary source of food.

Flowering plants suddenly appeared in the fossil record at about the same time that dinosaurs became extinct. For Charles Darwin, who depended on the fossil record to support his theory on evolution, this was an "abominable mystery." The new angiosperm groups were so numerous and complex that fundamentalist Christians pointed to them as proof of the biblical creation myth, a myth that was inherited from early Mesopotamian writings.

Philip Regal explains the angiosperm mystery as the emergence of a synergism between plants, pollinators, and seed dispersers that gave flowering plants the weaponry necessary to win the tropical assault for territory against gymnosperms, cycads, tree ferns, seed ferns, and ginkos. It was an ecological revolution as powerful as the linking of gunpowder with projectiles. The setting of Regal's theory takes us on a detour in time to when life had just emerged onto land from the seas.

During the long course of evolution, numerous revolutionary innovations have catapulted the planet's animal life into totally new arenas where they have had to adapt to very different ways of life. One of these adaptations was the acquisition of toothed jaws for capturing and killing large prey. Others were the development of legs, eyes, skin resistant to water loss, and the entire spectrum of adaptations necessary for marine organisms to exploit terrestrial life. Once on land, vertebrates encountered new habitats and had to reform again, first as reptiles and then as birds and mammals to become masters of the ground, underground, air, and sea.

These countless developments would not have taken place had it not been for plants. Aside from producing the food upon which land animals survived, plants set the stage for animal evolution and greatly influenced animal form, especially herbivores. The proboscis of a weevil, for instance, is designed for penetrating thick seed coats to reach the nut contained within. Similarly the long beak of a hummingbird reaches deep into a flower to gather hidden nectar reserves, and the giraffe has a form that resembles a tree; with its trunklike neck it can reach vegetation on high limbs.

The extent to which animal evolution is indebted to plants is seldom appreciated. Loren Eiseley, the quintessential naturalist, spoke of this in his book *The Immense Journey:*

> . . . The hand that grasped the stone by the river long ago would pluck a handful of grass seed and hold it contemplatively. In that moment, the golden towers of man, his swarming millions, his turning wheels, the vast learning of his packed libraries, would glimmer dimly there in the ancestor of wheat, a few seeds held in a muddy hand. Without the gift of flowers and the infinite diversity of their fruits, man and bird, if they had continued to exist at all, would be today unrecognizable. *Archaeopteryx*, the lizard-bird, might still be snapping at beetles on a sequoia limb; man might still be a nocturnal insectivore gnawing a roach in the dark. The weight of a petal has changed the face of the world and made it ours.

The dawn of terrestrial life can be traced back to the rudimentary beginnings of land plants in the late Silurian period, about 425 million years ago. Small plants closely related to algae were pioneering the wettest areas but all else remained barren. The plants had "crawled" prostrate onto land, their rubbery marine skeletons sagging under the strong pull of gravity. They did not, could not, venture far from very wet environments—swamps, seasides, rivers, and streams—because their mobile sperm needed plenty of water to search for fertile eggs.

In the early Devonian (about 400 million years ago) primitive plants began fighting gravitation with strong stems and vessels that carried nutrients to nascent leaves basking in the warm sun. A plant that fell behind in developing ways to reach into the air would be overshadowed and possibly killed by starvation. So began an aerial battle for light that is still being fought. Primitive plants, in terms of the long intervals of evolutionary time, quickly attained heights of many inches. This set the pace for scampering herbivores and predators that had followed plants from the seas. These animals were primarily terrestrial arthropods, a group composed of scorpions, spiders, centipedes, and predecessors to insects.

The embryonic beginning of the canopy in the Devonian, though it may not have been extremely complex or tall, was an evolutionary force that immediately went to work on herbivores. Olfactory clues no longer led walking insect ancestors on a straight path to food. To travel between the tops of two different plants, hungry herbivores would have to climb down branches to the ground, then up the stem of a neighbor, perhaps the wrong one, and along many different limbs until trial and error finally brought them to the correct location. These species would possibly have been the most intelligent of insects, for they would have had to evolve a brain that could decipher the maze of paths leading to food.

The greatest evolutionary pressure on insects came as plants continued their tendency to grow tall and began to diversify into club mosses, horsetails, and ferns. Their nutritious apical meristems, reproductive tissues, and leaves were being carried ever higher above the ground, out of reach for the nonclimber. The food sites at branch ends became separated by space just like polka dots on an inflating balloon. During a process that took tens of millions of years, the insects bridged these gaps and arrived at food sites with more and more proficiency by gradually progressing through hopping then gliding stages. Within this embryonic canopy was the impetus behind the conquest of air by primitive flying insects.

By the beginning of the Carboniferous period (350 million years ago) the short bushy plants of the Devonian had transformed into giants; club mosses and progymnosperms reached a hundred feet in height, while horsetails (sphenopsids) exceeded fifty feet. Dense forests of these plants covered continental-wide mires and shallows. This was the start of an eighty-million-year period of innovation, diversification, and increasing height for plants, and the corresponding elaboration and modification of animals occurred simultaneously.

Most textbooks make it difficult to imagine the conformation and ambiance of early forests. Pictures often depict horsetail trees, seed ferns, tree ferns, club mosses, and progymnosperms as standing isolated, no doubt to emphasize their structure, but for whatever reason, the effect has been wholly misleading. Drawings usually place these early trees in steppe, savanna, or desert conditions rather than the densely packed forest belts in which they are known to have lived. Evidence of the prolific junglelike growth of these plant assemblages is preserved in one of our most important resources— coal. (An excellent reconstruction of a Carboniferous forest basement is at the Chicago Museum of Natural History, reproduced in *Paleobotany* by William Darrah.)

It is wondrous to conceive of mid-Carboniferous jungles and tantalizing to speculate about the nature of the first mature canopy communities. To create an accurate likeness of a primeval forest, imagine the moss, lycopods, horsetails, and ferns of today's forests and glades tremendously enlarged. Some ferns, now extinct, were sixty to seventy feet tall, with trunks up to two feet in diameter; club mosses in at least two genera, *Lepidodendron* and *Sigillaria*, attained heights of between 130 and 170 feet. Trees of the Cordaitales, also entirely extinct, grew to one hundred feet tall. These were the largest members of Carboniferous forests and they were complemented by many more smaller species, forming a complex ecosystem about which almost nothing is known. In terms of height, the canopies of Carboniferous forests equaled anything that can now be found in the Amazon Basin, Central America, or Africa.

Yet the ancient forest was relatively monotonous. Colorful fruit and flowers that we take for granted had not yet evolved, which left only a dull spectrum of greens, grays, and browns. There were no seeds, nuts, pollen, or nectar. Tight clumps of tree ferns unfurled on their elevated stems. Tree crowns consisted of spreading branches covered by spiny leaves, and limbs and trunks were coated with scales. Vines did not exist. There were no fragrances, just acrid, paludal odors emanating from submerged and decaying vegetation. Hollow thumps and splashes from falling trees echoed as they hit the wet earth and water; winds rustled and sighed through coniferous limbs. Insects sang choruses like the songs of crickets and cicadas, and as they hovered above the water depositing eggs, fish jumped after them, dimpling the swamp's surface with expanding rings of wavelets. Wind-blown waves broke against shores and floating trunks. On a still day one might have heard the powerful jaws of an amphibian snap shut and the flutter of the paperlike wings of an escaping insect, or cockroaches shuffling across ground litter, shifting the debris. Amphibians then were largely silent, except perhaps for an occasional wispy squeak when they were caught by an adversary. It was a strange world dominated by now extinct plants and animals.

The Carboniferous has been called the age of amphibians, but it was also a time when insects were rapidly evolving. At their beginning, insects belonged to a few orders that are now mostly extinct, but by the end of the Carboniferous, in the Permian, they multiplied to at least twenty orders, which included lacewing flies, book lice, beetles, and flies. Many of these groups thrived and some became gigantic as they moved into unoccupied plant environments. Cockroaches, for example, attained six inches in length. The strangest transformation took place in the aerial jungle, where huge dragonflies filled the niche of nonexistent birds and bats. These had wingspans of two feet and were the largest insects of all time. Since dragonflies are adept at catching insects while flying, we are left to wonder what sizable species they pursued while navigating ancient canopy airways. The most notable group was cockroaches. Over six hundred species have been found, some of which no doubt lived in the canopy. If the Carboniferous can be called the age of amphibians, it most certainly was the age of cockroaches and insects as well.

Whether or not Carboniferous forests had epiphytes is a moot question. Modern tropical tree limbs hold numerous epiphyte representatives of ancient plant varieties such as ferns, liverworts, lichens, mosses, and club mosses. Therefore, it would be reasonable to presume that branches in the primitive canopy were similarly adorned with these plants. The arrival of plants capable of growing on tree limbs was a quantum leap in canopy complexity because epiphytes would have been the ecological base, both as food and shelter, for a wide range of additional insects. Scorpions, centipedes, and spiders must have numbered among the first canopy fauna. These predators probably searched out prey wherever it could be found, and it was unlikely they would remain content living on the forest floor.

We can only wonder if amphibians also wandered from the miry ground and climbed to the insect-dominated canopy. It seems possible that when amphibians were at their zenith in the late Carboniferous, one or more of the small salamanderlike microsaurians may have discovered that the rough scaly bark of certain ancient trees made ideal ladderlike footholds. The history of evolution suggests that almost anything is possible. Examples of this are the marsupials, primitive pouched mammals, of Australia. Once marsupials became isolated on the drifting island continent, where placental mammals were absent, they radiated into nearly every conceivable terrestrial and arboreal niche. There were marsupial dogs, cats, moles, flying squirrels, primates, rabbits, deer, mice, weasels, and more.

Frogs did not evolve until 100 million years later, in the Triassic period. This took place at pools on the ground where hopping, saltatorial locomotion evolved as a rapid way to evade predators. Saltation was exactly the adaptation that preadapted frogs for successful exploitation of treetops. We do not know when they became arboreal, but frogs are now important denizens of the canopy.

The last period of the Carboniferous, the Permian (230–200 million years ago), was marked by cooling climates and intense glaciation, conditions that must have played havoc with the "hothouse" tree varieties of the Carboniferous because new plant associations appear in its fossil beds. There is some confusion as to what did happen at that time since the Permian was also when reptiles arose. Neither reptiles nor the dominant amphibians of the Permian were noted for their cold-weather durability. That they survived and proliferated throughout this period suggests that tropical and subtropical conditions did not totally vanish; warm lowland jungles probably flourished in limited areas.

It was during the Permian that reptiles probably entered the canopy. These explorers belonged to a now extinct group, the lizard-like eosuchians. Like the amphibians that may have invaded aerial habitats, these reptiles perhaps were able to climb the rough scaly bark of late Carboniferous trees. Even if eosuchians themselves did not become arboreal, it was the destiny of their offspring. The descendants of these primitive reptiles were the Archosauria, which in later periods gave rise to large, bipedal dinosaurs such as *Tyrannosaurus*, flying reptiles, birds, crocodilians, and *Hypsilophodon*, a bipedal dinosaur that seemed well-adapted to arboreal life.

The early Permian was a time of drastic change. Land beneath the continent-sized swamps and marshes began uplifting as blocks of the earth's crust migrated and collided. This drained the lowlands upon which Carboniferous forests dwelt and large horsetails, club mosses, and many ferns were not able to colonize the emerging land areas. These plants had a vital need for nearby mates and very wet conditions were necessary for them to successfully disperse their aquatic, microscopic sperm.

Just as reptiles succeeded in escaping swamplands, gymnosperms and pteridosperms were able to colonize dry ground. The innovation of seeds and pollen freed these "advanced" plants from wet environments. Throughout the Permian the numbers of species possessing these innovations must have grown and transformed the canopy into a vast aerial zone of stored seed energy. And this must have led to yet another quantum leap in canopy complexity. A broader range of insect species was supported as well as larger populations, all seeking the relative lavishness of treetop life.

To understand the gymnosperm's highly successful life cycle we can look at a fern to see where gymnosperms have come from. Ferns have a life cycle involving two plants that appear to be totally dissimilar. One is a thumbnail-sized gametophyte that rests close to the damp earth and the other is a sporophyte, the plant we all recognize as a fern. The gametophyte is made of very delicate tissue that produces both swimming sperm (which shrivel and die out of water) and immobile eggs. Gametophytes can easily become desiccated. They need water to remain vigorous and splashing rain to disperse their sperm. After fertilization the sporophyte begins growing within the gametophyte's tissue. It becomes larger and larger and finally sends roots into the ground, after which the gametophyte dies. Ferns are found only in or near conditions favorable to water-loving gametophytes. In the case of conifers, for example, gymnosperms did away with the gametophyte phase by putting male gametophytes in tiny floating pollen grains and female gametophytes inside cones. Gymnosperm pollen was an invention equivalent to that of internal fertilization in reptiles, while seeds were analogous to reptilian eggs. These adaptations finally helped to bridge the barriers that had hitherto prevented plants from colonizing all of earth's land areas.

Sperm packed in wind-borne pollen had another advantage for gymnosperms: it offered a greater variety of mates. Our temperate evergreen gymnosperm forests serve as models for what may have happened in ancient forests. In spring and summer, when conifers produce pollen, it can often be seen rising in dense clouds from forests. Much of this pollen travels hundreds of miles. In contrast, more primitive plants of the Carboniferous were obligated to mate with the plant next door. In plants especially, this can be incestuous, which is detrimental.

Vast expanses of Carboniferous forests disappeared in the Permian and Triassic periods, but canopy communities must have thrived in the areas where tropical forests persisted. Leaving the Paleozoic era and moving into the Mesozoic, earth's treetops became even more important food sites as species having seeds and pollen continued to proliferate. The stage was set for the invasion of the canopy by reptiles.

Edwin H. Colbert, in his book *The Age of Reptiles*, tells where reptiles could be found: "There were large reptiles and small ones, plant-eating types and meat-eaters that fed upon the herbivores. Some reptiles lived on high ground, some along the rivers, some in the trees."

As has been said, the first arboreal reptiles were possibly the eosuchians, or one of their small archosaurian descendants. These animals, like the insects that preceded them, must have begun jumping between limbs in pursuit of insects and other reptiles and were no less susceptible to the canopy's molding forces.

How these forces might have shaped early reptiles was shown to me in 1978 when I saw some rather impressive aerial prowess in a species of anole lizard while at 130 feet above the ground in a

Hymenolobium (not the same tree holding *Gnetum*). One anole scaled a nearby branch and prepared to launch itself toward a distant limb. (These lizards typically do a lot of jumping.) Noticing that there was a cross wind blowing, which the lizard would have to allow for, I watched with a good deal of interest. The anole set off on a course toward the limb. It flattened its abdomen, apparently to improve its glide, corrected for the wind, and arrived on target. Over a span of several minutes two more anoles followed the first along the same route with identical accuracy. Sometime later I saw an anole dive straight down to escape my net, then pull into a graceful, gliding arc that carried it on a more or less horizontal course back to the trunk that held the limb from which it had started.

It is an interesting and revealing statement of our knowledge about earth's fossil life to note that if these anoles became fossilized, future scientists would never know they were arboreal, nor would the anole's features give this fact away. Our ignorance about extinct fossil species is overwhelming, so we must keep an open mind toward where they may have lived and what their habits might have been. We should expect that many species in ancient canopies were similar to anoles in that they also were on the threshold of gliding. This is certainly true today because there are a large number of species, including snakes, lizards, frogs, squirrels, and marsupials, that have more or less well-developed means for gliding.

It is a change of behavior that sets the stage for evolution, a type of change depicted by the behavior of the anoles. If the anoles' ribs participated in making the abdomen flat, this species could eventually have wings. A living example of this can be found in the jungle canopies of the East Indies and Malay Archipelago. It is a lizard called *Draco volans*, or "flying dragon." They are diminutive and were it not for ample documentation, one might expect them to be a sideshow fabrication. Their wings expand outward from the abdomen, leaving the front and hind legs completely free, a form reminiscent of an angel. The wings do not have heavy musculature for powered flight, but are rather unique in that they are supported by ribs. *Draco* lizards are renowned for being able to glide for long distances and occasionally may perform an acrobatic loop-de-loop. The evolution of these lizards began a long time ago in a fashion very similar to that of the anole lizards of La Selva's canopy.

Everet Olson, a vertebrate paleontologist at UCLA, once pulled a journal from his collection and opened it to a page depicting a fossil. It was an early record of a gliding vertebrate, a small dinosaur, and it had an uncanny likeness to *Draco*. The extinct species was not at all closely related to *Draco*, which demonstrates the incredible consistency of canopy forces. Two unrelated species, separated by a vast span of time, have been sculpted into a nearly identical form.

While reptiles experimented with invading the sky, several of their lineages filled other habitats. Huge whalelike icthyosaurs, smaller nothosaurs, and plesiosaurs chased fish in the shallow seas, while dinosaurs of all sizes and mammal-like reptiles ranged about the land.

It was during the Triassic that plants in the gymnosperm group, Bennettitales, began evolving another structure, the flower. We do not know where or under exactly what circumstances this took place, but a hypothetical example may serve to show how flowers, one of the most significant advances of evolution, may have come about.

The Bennettitales were not large plants, which suggests that they could have inhabited the basements of primitive tropical forests. A living genera related to this group, *Zamia*, is a ground plant that does quite well in perpetual shade. Like modern jungles, winds must have been very light in primitive basement environments. For a wind-pollinated plant to be reproductively successful, it would have to have been located close to others of its kind to take advantage of the slightest air movement.

The primitive basement would have had its share of pollinating insects that no doubt were incidental pollinators long before flowers originated. This was the major evolutionary force giving rise to flowers. Insects would have flown between most pollen-producing plants more or less regularly to satisfy their hunger, and during the process pollen would have rubbed off and stuck on their bodies. Plants "placed" their female reproductive parts near the anthers, where insects would be more likely to bump against the pollen-covered organs. Cross-pollination resulted whenever one of these insects came into contact with a different plant's female reproductive organs. Over time, and with the addition of petals as colorful invitations to pollen feasts, the flower emerged. The linkup with

My four-by-eight-foot observation platform 111 feet above the ground in a monkey pot tree.

THE PLATFORM

Motmot with katydid.

Red-lored parrot.

Transparent "glass" frog *Centrolenella*.

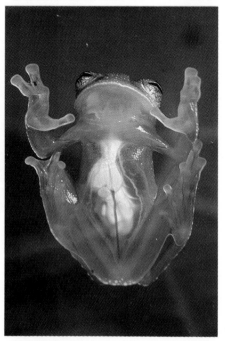

Two-toed sloth.

Three-toed sloth.

Tree frog, *Agalychnis calcarifer*.

VISITORS
IN THE VICINITY
OF THE PLATFORM

Sunrise over lowland rain forest.

Great potoo. This is the first photograph of this bird in the wild.

Moth that came to a candle.

Tiny hawk; to my knowledge the
only photograph of this bird in
the wild.

Howler monkey; mother and young visit the platform.

A tree frog sitting on an orchid next to my cot.

Large spider with a three- to four-inch
leg span that lived on my platform.
Egg case of the above species.

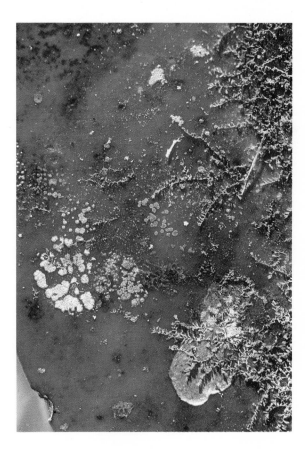

Leaf of epiphyte with moss. As in the
ocean, all surfaces develop an encrust-
ing layer of life.

Rare bromeliad and, beyond, a volcanic mountain chain of the Caribbean slope.

insects was a potentially formidable new evolutionary weapon that gave plants the ability to mate where winds were insufficient. Yet, and this is part of Regal's theory, without a more effective means of dispersing seeds to distant locations, such as widely spaced light gaps, and without an escape from the many seed eaters near the parent plant, flowers by themselves would not have been capable of deposing flowerless gymnosperms. Flowering plants had to wait tens of millions of years for a new and quicker means of seed dispersal. They had to wait for the canopy to again work its magic.

While flowers made their historical union with insects, reptiles were still crawling among limbs and jumping after insects. The *Draco*-like glider was only one of many reptiles that had probably invaded the canopy. From one of these other types, the earliest advanced aerial vertebrate appeared: it was a pterosaur, up to three feet long, found in the lower Jurassic shales of Europe. Edwin H. Colbert writes in *The Age of Reptiles:*

> [Dimorphodon, a pterosaur,] was one of the earliest animals to attempt true flight. It is, in spite of its somewhat clumsy appearance, a highly specialized animal, that bespeaks a most interesting evolutionary history bridging the gap from ground-living or tree-dwelling reptiles to fully fledged flying types, a history of which there is not the slightest trace to be found in the rocks.

A problem arises when we try to imagine how *Dimorphodon* came to possess wings. Fossil pterosaurs are often associated with marine species such as plesiosaurs and ichthyosaurs. It is generally assumed that these pterosaurs lived on cliffs where they could take advantage of prevailing winds and wind lift not readily available in forests. There, they plied the seacoast breeze and caught fish in their long, toothy jaws.

The origin of this reptile's wings can only be guessed. If the pterosaur precursor, which originated from a thecodont ancestor, was the same size as *Dimorphodon* when it began evolving flight, we would have to hypothesize a very restricted manner in which it developed. The falling-mouse-and-man problem shows that a large animal cannot propel itself through air and then land safely without having a very large wing membrane. Man and hang glider are a case in point. Experimenting with rudimentary flight membranes would have been fatal unless the landing site was relatively soft. Early pterosaurs may have attained their adaptations at cliffs near the seashore and refined them over ages of diving from perches to catch fish. Their wings could have gradually evolved as aiming mechanisms. That the proto-pterosaurs could have been divers is suggested by iguanas of the New World that dive from high limbs into rivers and also are known to dive from low cliffs for algae in the Galapagos Islands. This would have been a novel way for flight to have evolved.

H. G. Seeley, in *Dragons of the Air*, leaves open the possibility of a more likely route:

> Dimorphodon . . . is associated with evidences of terrestrial land animals, the best known of which is Sceli-dosaurus, an armored Dinosaur adapted by its limbs for progression on land. And the Pterodactyl Campylognathus . . . is associated with trunks of coniferous trees and re-mains of Insects. So that the occurrence of Pterodactyles in a marine stratum is not inconsistent with their having been transported by streams off the old land surface of the Lias, on which coniferous trees grew and Dinosaurs lived.

I believe an arboreal route was most likely, as does J. Marvin Weller in his book *The Course of Evolution:* "These creatures prob-ably evolved from a line of small unknown thecodonts that had adapted to arboreal habits. Flight is believed to have originated with climbing animals which had acquired structures permitting them to glide from tree to tree."

It seems safe to speculate that large seacoast pterosaurs evolved from smaller pterosaurs. The smaller body size fits what would be expected for animals that went through a dangerous gliding stage in the canopy. Later fossils support this possibility. Many small pterodactyls have been found—one no larger than a sparrow. The fact that these small varieties have not been found in Triassic fossil beds previous to Dimorphodon is a matter of probability, as they surely existed in the jungles that crowded the coast.

Once gliding developed, pterosaurs moved into new habitats where they increased in size. A wingspan of more than a few feet would have been a detriment in the canopy, although probably large-winged, carrion-eating pterosaurs existed then, just as today's forests have vultures. It would seem more plausible that smaller species with faster aerial responses inhabited forest canopies where they steered through limbs and treetops, while larger, less maneuverable species, some with wingspans in excess of thirty feet, lived near the sea and in other unobstructed habitats. In open areas, the danger of striking a limb and damaging a wing bone were nearly nonexistent, and there were also more reliable winds to facilitate flight for lumbering species.

Pterosaurs, like the Wright brothers' first airplane, were not great fliers—great gliders probably, but not fliers. They lacked a keeled sternum, upon which powerful wing muscles attach; without one of these, a reptile could have only rudimentary powered flight. They also apparently lacked insulation such as feathers or fur and in all probability were "cold-blooded." For all their magnificence, pterosaurs had a limited ecological role; they probably ate insects, fish, and decomposing dinosaurs. Fibrous vegetation would not have held the energy reserves required by such agile and active reptiles. While it is true that seeds and pollen had brought concentrated energy sources into the canopy, these sources still were not abundant enough to support a large community of warm-blooded fliers. Many seeds were protected by gymnosperm cones and were available only to specialized insects and ground-dwelling dinosaurs.

Even though pterosaurs were efficient gliders, they were doomed by a rival species who also began experimenting with flight. Loren Eiseley observed in an earlier quote that "the weight of a petal has changed the face of the world and made it ours." There is, however, a more fundamental invention that has formed the cornerstone of present-day ecology: feathers. Feathers were first used for gliding and flight; they then took on the function of insulation, which promoted warm-bloodedness. This created the possibility for a new biological economy between plant and reptile that when instituted would mean the death of all pterosaurs, dinosaurs, and the plants these animals depended on.

The earliest fossil feather was reported in 1861 and came from an aerial reptile known as *Archaeopteryx*. The fossil, found in Upper Jurassic shales, was not considered to be authentic at first, but once it was accepted, conservative elements of the scientific community were confounded. Was it a "reptilian bird" or a "feathered reptile"? The confusion may seem odd to those of us who appreciate the process of evolution, but at that time Wallace and Darwin had only recently published their theory and there were those who were not yet convinced of its validity. It makes no difference what *Archaeopteryx* was called because we now know it was a perfect example of a "missing evolutionary link" the creature had developed to a point midway between a gliding and flying stage. This type of fossil has never been found for insects.

Attached to *Archaeopteryx* is a baffling evolutionary enigma. Its feathers, which are identical to those of modern birds, give no hint as to how they evolved from reptilian scales. Some biologists have suggested that feathers first originated as insulation to keep reptiles warm, or they evolved on terrestrial reptiles as nets to trap insects, then later were applied to flight. A combination of these two theories has been proposed by John Ostrom and has received attention in *The New York Times* "Science" section. However, a paper published in *Science* (1979) by Alan Feduccia and Harrison B. Tordorff has helped to put both these ideas to rest. The authors concluded that *Archaeopteryx* feathers "evolved in the selective context of flight." Neither an insulative function nor the suggested use as insect nets can explain the aerodynamic structure of feathers. It is once again widely accepted that *Archaeopteryx* developed as a glider with nominal powers of flight in tropical or subtropical tree-tops.

It is known that feathers originated from reptilian scales, but the evolutionary process by which they became flight structures is still in question. Feathers probably began as enlarged scales, or aerodynamic fringes, that increased the surface-lift area of leaping arboreal lizards. Fringes are widespread structures of today's gliders; some are made of hair, or more commonly skin, such as is found in flying squirrels. A hint that feathers originated in this fashion is seen when looking at the gliding gecko lizard of the Asian tropics. It has enlarged scales fringing its body that slow its fall and probably enhance maneuverability while the lizard glides.

The ancestral scale fringe of *Archaeopteryx* was a fringe with a difference. The scales grew into perfect structures of flight by being both strong and incredibly light. Rather quickly, I imagine, feathers became aerodynamic flaps to lift the reptile with an efficiency unmatched by any other glider. With the arrival of *Archaeopteryx*, feathers had improved to the point of being nearly identical to modern asymmetrical flight feathers, which act as one-way valves, opening to allow the wing to be effortlessly lifted, then closing for the power stroke of flight. The feathers functioned to increase travel dramatically within the primitive canopy domain. At this stage they probably did not function as insulation, as *Archaeopteryx*, like the pterosaurs with which it shared the treetop habitat, was probably little better than a cold-blooded glider. Yet in the construction of this ancient prototype there was room for fantastic refinement.

Evolving birds had to break a reptilian barrier that hindered effective flight before they could become vehicles for the demise of dinosaurs and the rise of mammals. Reptile muscles tire quickly because heavy exercise produces waste, lactic acid, at a higher rate than it can be processed. This is why a lizard will become immobile after a short period of running. The animal literally cannot run anymore and a very long rest is needed for recovery. There is no indication that *Archaeopteryx* strayed far from this reptilian mode.

For the canopy to successfully restructure *Archaeopteryx* into an aerial machine, it was necessary for the animals' engines to evolve. Feathers were not simply airfoils, they were the beginning of the best insulating material known, excepting a vacuum. Proliferating layers of feathers and developing flight muscles began to transform the gliding lizard into a high-performance mechanism. This mechanism can be crudely compared to a steam engine: make a bigger fire and the train moves faster. Feathers increased body temperature by acting like a Thermos to retard escaping heat. This ultimately made it possible for metabolic fires to maintain a high and constant body temperature (endothermic-homoiothermy). Attainment of warm-bloodedness in birds is probably linked solely to the refinement of weak-powered flight.

There were some important reasons why powered and sustainable flight would have been under constant pressure for improvement. Perhaps *Archaeopteryx* specialized in gliding from limbs to attack prey near the ground and then ran, flew, and climbed to return to a perch and/or glided and flew between tree crowns where there was much insect activity. The beginnings of homoiothermy accelerated the removal of lactic acid from muscles and gave rapid recovery from flight fatigue. This facilitated longer and longer flights and brought new food sites into range, along with an improved ability to escape from predators. Prolonged flight would have been especially important near the ground, where gliding to safety was impossible.

Even partial homoiothermy would have been accompanied by a high energy bill, as those who have tried to keep a northern house at 70 degrees year-round know. It seems there was a limit to how many early birds could be supported by the energy-poor Jurassic and early Cretaceous forests. So as primitive birds became warmblooded they remained rare except near the sea, where concentrated energy for powered flight was contained in fish. Compared to even a partially warm-blooded species, cold-blooded pterosaurs had a much lower metabolic rate and needed much less nourishment to stay alive, so one would expect that even in forests they would be more common than primitive warm-blooded birds.

In the early Cretaceous (120 million years ago) nearly all the essential actors of the coming revolution were present. The flora and fauna were an odd mixture of old and new. Hungry primitive birds flapped feebly into the skies; pterosaurs glided high over hills, mountains, and cliffs; large and small dinosaurs roamed the earth; and small, ravenous mammals stalked insects at night. A few species of primitive flowering plants and their insect pollinators inhabited the canopy and basement habitats of jungles that were dominated by tree ferns and gymnosperms such as cycads, gingkos, and conifers. According to Regal's theory, this scene would change near the end of the Cretaceous as flowering plants forged their new ecological relationship with birds. This relationship would create a phenomenal boost in the available food sources of the planet.

A new form of energy was beginning to materialize, almost out of thin air, through coevolutionary processes. Feathered, gliding reptiles gave birth to birds that had an ever-increasing need for energetic foods to fuel increasingly powerful flight muscles. Voracious appetites due to increasing metabolic rates made primitive birds reliable visitors to angiosperms, where they found swarms of insects around flowers and seeds. The exact time when seeds of flowering plants gained a nutritious covering is not known, but by the close of the first half of the Cretaceous a solid link seems to have been forged between birds and evolving fruit. To attract birds, plants provided easily digestible energy packets in the form of concentrated sugar. After being lured in, a bird could be exploited; seeds would stick to feathers, bills, feet, or were swallowed, then carried off to favorable growth sites. The potent ecological consequence of this relationship was that angiosperms were becoming the planet's major power source for the evolution of terrestrial, arboreal, and aerial warm-blooded animals.

Just as mankind's capacity to use the "free" energy of coal and oil has brought rapid cultural change, the formulation of a new ecological energy equation shook the foundation of ancient life. The dominant, primitive plants of lowland jungles that relied on less effective wind dispersal began to disappear as angiosperm seeds were transported quickly to any spot in the forest. As old gymnosperms fell and formed gaps, angiosperms were the first arrivals to colonize them. Bird-dispersed seeds also helped angiosperms to escape seed-eating insects and other predators that congregated below tree crowns. Gymnosperm seeds that were wind-dispersed and relatively immobile became easy victims of seed predators. Pollination by insects helped angiosperms maintain reproduction between mates in distantly located gaps. Birds, flowering plants, and insects acted in unison to intensify each other's effectiveness. Together they catapulted earth's terrestrial ecosystem into a dynamic era of evolution.

By the late Cretaceous (60 million years ago) angiosperms increased in number and were diversifying into all available niches. As angiosperms continued to proliferate, gymnosperms were forced to become more widely spaced. Ultimately, this meant that wind pollination, which depended on dense populations of the same species, would fail. Primitive plants, the basis of the food web, were becoming extinct and taking reptilian herbivores and their monstrous predators with them. Over a period of tens of millions of years the dinosaurs and gymnosperms were pushed to extinction; the age of birds, angiosperms, and mammals had begun. (Contrary to popular belief, there is no evidence that dinosaurs became extinct abruptly. The evidence that does exist suggests that dinosaurs disappeared over a period of many millions of years.)

The age of mammals in itself has been a major biological puzzle. Many scientists outside of ecology have been reluctant to accept the fact that competitive interactions can and do change the earth's biotic face. They claim that, if mammals were superior to reptiles, they would have replaced dinosaurs in the early Cretaceous or Jurassic. Instead primitive mammals lived alongside them for tens of millions of years as small insectivores. Comparing reptiles to mammals is like comparing apples and oranges; they are not ecological equivalents. There is no reason to suppose that mammals were superior to reptiles but rather that reptiles were much better fitted to the overall biotic environment of their time. The question is not why did mammals live alongside reptiles without coming to dominate them, but *what* environmental factors stopped mammals from proliferating.

Mammals in a sense were waiting for a ripe opportunity to evolve. Like birds, mammals had become warm-blooded before the arrival of angiosperms and "found" themselves in an energy-poor world where resources were suited to cold-blooded (ectotherms) reptiles. High fiber, leafy diets of the time lacked the nutrition needed by today's large and small mammalian herbivores and there is little reason to think that primitive mammals would have been any different. For example, the leafy diets of ungulates such as deer, cattle, sheep, pigs, and horses are supplemented with grains. Without grain and other angiosperm products, large warm-blooded herbivores would find survival impossible.

Sloths and koala bears are good examples of how a strict leaf-eating diet affects the mammalian metabolism. A sloth's metabolism operates at 42 percent of the expected rate for a mammal of its size. Sloths cannot digest food fast enough to always maintain high body temperatures, so on cold days their temperatures fall several degrees. A similar condition exists for koala bears. To subsist on leaves, these warm-blooded animals have undergone reverse evolution; by partially giving up homoiothermy, they have taken a step toward becoming cold-blooded. The hoatzin, a bird of the Amazon Basin that exists on a leafy diet, has nearly lost the ability of powered flight. This suggests that diet and the amount of energy that could be extracted from prehistoric food played an integral part in determining the type of organisms that came to populate the earth. Gymnosperm leaves and other dominant vegetation prior to the late Cretaceous were notably more fibrous and less edible than grass, shrubs, and tree leaves. This strengthens the conclusion that ancient forest vegetation would have been a poor springboard to widespread warm-bloodedness even among birds. In those times warm-bloodedness was fueled only by eating insects, scavenging and living near the sea or lakes where fish were plentiful. As a result mammals could not become large-bodied elements of ancient terrestrial vertebrate communities.

Why then didn't dinosaur-eating mammals—carnivores—evolve in the Jurassic? Some recent discoveries about tropical American carnivores perhaps supply an answer. Daniel Janzen, in his book *Costa Rican Natural History*, states that tropical carnivores are highly frugivorous. "The . . . Carnivora [of Costa Rica] comprise six felids, two canids, six species of procyonid, and seven species of mustilid. All except the otter (*Lutra longicaudus*) and mountain lion (*Felis concolor*) are known or alleged to consume large amounts of fruit." These animals are excellent dispersers since their intestines do little damage to seeds. Fruit has probably always been an important part of carnivore diets and these animals may have been able to evolve solely because of the growing availability of fruit and highly nutritious leaves after the late Cretaceous when angiosperms were diversifying. It is highly probable that a paucity of readily digestible plant parts that were packed with energy kept all types of mammals and birds, except insectivores, rare and unimportant in ancient times.

This view of ancient forests as being energy poor also explains another feature of dinosaurian biology. A direct extrapolation from our knowledge about mammalian body size versus food quality provides a possible reason why dinosaurs tended to be large. For thermodynamic and physical reasons it is known that as animals become larger, they are more able to process large volumes of low-quality food to survive. Thus, the largest herbivorous mammals also tend to eat the poorest foods. So it is not surprising that the largest terrestrial herbivores of all time fed on plant communities that were notably much more fibrous and of lower food quality than today's angiosperms (grasses are angiosperms).

With the arrival of angiosperms and birds at the end of the Cretaceous, a new age had begun for mammals. Immediately the forest canopy was invaded by a small, shrewlike insectivore whose descendants would become primates and bats. Under the unique selective pressures of the canopy, the former led to mankind and the latter followed a well-trodden path to become aerial animals. Bats were the third canopy animals to attain true flight, and today in any given New World jungle there are more species of bat, many of them frugivorous, than all other mammal groups together.

Regal's theory, with minor elaboration, is better than any other in explaining the complex ecological events that must have taken place during the late Cretaceous. Other theories do not incorporate the large amount of knowledge that has been gleaned from studies of tropical biology over the past twenty years. But to be credible a theory must systematically account for past and future biotic changes.

Regal knew that not all forest gymnosperms were pushed out of the tropics during the angiosperm-bird revolution. In the New World, for example, *Gnetum* and a ground plant known as *Zamia*, as well as a few other species, were survivors, and when Regal wrote his paper the natural histories of these relic gymnosperms were unknown. If it could be shown that these plants were able to survive the Cretaceous extinctions with both primitive gymnosperm adaptations—seeds and pollen dispersed by wind—his theory would be weakened.

My first observations of *Gnetum* in the crown of the giant *Hymenolobium* had been inconclusive concerning the plant's reproductive biology. Another opportunity to study the plant came a couple of years later when I again visited La Selva. Then David Clark, the station manager, told me *Zamia* was pollinated by insects and probably dispersed by ground mammals. This fit nicely into Regal's theory because *Zamia* had survived in the jungle by possessing angiosperm features and I immediately became anxious to see whether *Gnetum* had done the same.

At the time there was only one record that suggested what animal might disperse *Gnetum* seeds: monkeys. But this seemed unlikely because monkeys would probably relish the edible nut and do much more destruction than dispersal. To collect more data I again climbed the *Hymenolobium*.

By late afternoon white-faced monkeys appeared in trees next to mine, but because they are shy and alert animals I did not find out if their tastes included *Gnetum* seeds. The monkeys immediately detected my presence, barked harshly in alarm, and vanished into distant treetops.

There was much bird activity in and around the *Hymenolobium*, which kept my expectations high. Snowy cotingas and masked tityras, both canopy species, flew among the *Hymenolobium* limbs in search of insects. Three great green macaws landed in a tree about seventy yards away and ate fruit. These macaws were once common on the Atlantic slope but because of human activity they are now threatened by extinction. A white-necked puffbird sat on one of *Gnetum*'s vines and occasionally flew to catch a large insect in midair. The size of the prey that can be eaten whole by white-necked puffbirds is astounding; I was once five feet away from a puffbird that swallowed a cicada as large as its head. Flocks of parrots flew below and I had the unique opportunity of seeing their colorful dorsal plumage. A flock of crested guans, large turkey-like birds, flew one after another onto the limbs of a neighboring tree; they rested only momentarily before gliding to an unknown congregation point. The most spectacular visitor was an ornate hawk-eagle that landed twenty feet overhead. Like the great green macaw, the bird is rare and I felt fortunate to have gotten a close look at it. But none of these birds showed any interest in *Gnetum*'s sugary fruit and I was beginning to think that perhaps monkeys were the dispersers after all.

The day had been warm and I welcomed an arriving black-bottomed cloud and the cool rain it brought. The storm grabbed the *Hymenolobium* crown and shook its limbs furiously, sending me on a hair-raising ride. With the first sprinkle of rain, a rainbow gleamed over nearby forest, but unlike other rainbows its arc did not meet the ground. Because of the tree's height, the normal half-circle rainbow formed a full circle. This faded when heavy rain began spattering the treetop and soon a canopy deluge sent rivulets down the tree's branches soaking every square inch of bark and filling the tank of a stunningly beautiful bromeliad.

Following the rain, a male and female blue dacnis flew into the crown. They flitted between small branches overhead and I wondered what had gained their attention. The female disappeared into a hollow of the limb and water splashed out. In a few seconds she flew to a perch and the male hopped in. The birds were bathing in an arboreal tub where water had collected in a small hollow. I thought this was an uncommon event, but the following day a friend, Roberta Halsey, visited the tree and reported that two collared aracari toucans had bathed simultaneously in a larger hole on a lower part of the tree. The *Hymenolobium* was a canopy birdbath.

Time was running out for observations so I began preparing to leave. Two collared aracari toucans landed in the *Gnetum*'s branches and immediately began hunting for fruit. One of the birds selected a ripe fruit, chewed on it for a moment, hopped to another branch, and dropped the seed to the basement. This was a disappointing example of dispersal; a falling seed that ricocheted off a limb would have been just as good. The other toucan handled a seed similarly, and after several minutes they mysteriously fled, empty-mouthed.

The sun edged closer to the horizon and I was about to descend when another, much larger toucan entered the tree. It was a chestnut-mandibled toucan, the largest of La Selva's toucans. Within seconds the bird hopped sideways down a branch to a clump of *Gnetum* leaves and fruits. I waited unmoving, my heartbeat elevated with excitement, not wanting to scare the bird away. It was closely inspecting the fruits several feet above my head. After a moment it pulled a ripe fruit free and made many deep cuts into the flesh with its bill. Then to my astonishment the majestic bird tossed the fruit into the air. With a wide-open beak pointed straight up, the toucan caught the falling seed and swallowed it like a piece of popcorn. It did this another time before flying away.

Toucans are high-quality dispersers of seeds constructed like those of the *Gnetum*. The bird cuts the fruit before swallowing so that its muscular crop, located in the esophagus, has an easier time removing the sweet covering. Afterward the bird spits up the unharmed seeds at distant sites in the forest. The chestnut-mandibled toucan seems to have coevolved with *Gnetum* fruit, a possibility that became obvious in hindsight. *Gnetum* appears to have survived the Cretaceous extinctions by adopting the angiosperm ecological strategy; it, too, offered energy-rich food to birds in exchange for effective dispersal.

One bit of natural history remained to be illuminated: the

nature of *Gnetum*'s pollination system. Since the vines were somewhat rare and separated by many hundreds of yards, it seemed that wind pollination would not be effective. One might predict that *Gnetum* would have "flowers" to allure possible animal pollinators, but this was not the case. The female reproductive structures lacked anything that resembled a flower or nectar, without which it was difficult to imagine what would attract pollinators.

Nevertheless there was substantial evidence that viable seeds were being produced; the forest floor under *Gnetum* was crammed with seedling vines struggling to reach the canopy. A closer look at several fruiting stems gave a clue as to how *Gnetum* may reproduce. All the sites where fruit could develop had a tiny developing seed. Typically, tropical plants need pollen from another individual, and only a very small fraction of ovules produce fruit, except in plants that are capable of pollinating themselves. These often have high fruit production relative to the number of ovules. The extremely high seed set in *Gnetum* led me to suspect that it produced seed in the absence of sexual union, a condition known as apomixis in plants and parthenogenesis in animals. Even though the reproductive method of *Gnetum* remains an unresolved mystery, the fact that it is dispersed by the chestnut-mandibled toucan adds predictive substance to Regal's theory. Changing climates, due to long-term sun and earth cycles, and drifting continents may have helped set the stage for the extinctions of the late Cretaceous, but it was the elbow-to-elbow interactions described by Regal that turned over the ancient ecosystem, replacing it with one that still functions today.

The Treetop
Platform

BETWEEN 1974 AND 1978 jungles
were falling at rates that exceeded
the bleak estimate of tropical botanist Paul Richards; he predicted
that they would virtually disappear by the year 2000. During that
same period, my rope methods cracked the door to canopy research,
but it was a door that opened very slowly and only a handful of
biologists worldwide began to explore treetops. As each year passed
the magnitude of the work that lay ahead became increasingly in-
surmountable; that the canopy's story could fill a hundred thousand
hefty technical volumes, not one of which had been written. With
treetop life being exterminated each day, it seemed we were in
danger of leaving ourselves and future generations ignorant about
the most complex communities of life that have ever inhabited the
planet.

Since the world's population of "mainstream" biologists had
avoided canopy research because of the risk, I planned to devise a
"risk-free" way to study jungle treetops. The more people who saw

and understood the potential scientific and economic wealth of forests, the more likely they would be saved. In late June of 1978 an idea came to me for an exciting and safer way to explore treetops, one that I hoped would attract researchers and propel canopy biology toward becoming the major field of science that it deserves to be.

I had left the station after breakfast with enough equipment, bedding, and supplies to stay overnight in the canopy. My destination was a wooden platform in the crown of a monkey pot tree (*Lecythis ampla*) that I had recently constructed with the help of Mike Grayum and Phil DeVries, a butterfly biologist.

The day began auspiciously at seventy feet above ground where I met a three-toed sloth, *Bradypus variegatus*, resting in the crotch of a *Virola* tree. I raced to assemble an electronic flash on a camera as the sloth began climbing deliberately up the trunk. After several shots, it hid behind some leaves. The animal's fur was laced with green algae, which made it look like a mass of epiphytes or a large dangling fruit. A dead branch scraped its fur and a half dozen pyralid moths, perpetual residents of the living pelt, fled the disturbance, circling over the sloth's shoulder. The fur of these animals is also known to house mites, certain beetles, and several kinds of arthropods. It seems odd that they would be so thoroughly overrun with commensal organisms; over 900 beetles can be found on a given sloth.

Every day brought subtle changes to the surroundings. Several weeks earlier a large, white flower hung from an arboreal cactus that crept up a *Pentaclethra* trunk and spiraled around a major limb. The flower had now turned into a bright, red fruit. Small birds, especially ubiquitous euphonias, were attracted by the color and carried the sticky black seeds to other limbs where they might grow. Directly behind me some large, fleshy flowers dangled like ornaments from the stalk of a bignone vine. Euglossine bees, brilliant jewels with red and green bodies, hovered by flower entrances waiting their turn to enter. They are commonly called golden bees because of the twenty-four-karat metallic sheen of a few species; however, the group's colors range across the spectrum. Golden bees play more than an aesthetic role as they are the primary pollinators of both trees and epiphytes in the dim basement.

Climbing higher, above the *Virola* and nearby *Pentaclethras*, I felt the twinge of fear one encounters when rising into the relatively empty space separating crowns of tall trees from their shorter neighbors. When I began to climb, I had blindly accepted this fear as a logical and well-understood aspect of working at heights. Experience gradually revealed that what is called "the fear of heights" is actually a complex response having innate elements whose origins can be traced back to the time when our ancestors lived in the canopy.

On the ground one might expect that increasing height would simply result in increasing fear. However, the response I observed is more complicated and involves a multiplicity of known and previously unknown factors. This discovery was long in development and grew from introspection of my own feelings and through observing the responses of many scientists, bird-watchers, and tourists that climbed into the canopy. Everyone's fear followed a more or less identical pattern, a vacillation between feelings of illogical comfort and unreasonable fear. The following is an example of how a typical climber responded on a trip to the platform.

Novice rope climbers showed their first anxiety around fifteen feet, which was where one emerged through a layer of palm leaves into the aerial forest; it was also where height began to appear dangerous. The rope then passed near or through tree crowns up to a height of about seventy-five feet. During this leg of the climb everyone expressed growing concern, as would be expected, but at the same time they were undaunted in their resolve to reach the platform. Ten feet higher, at eighty-five feet, the local environment abruptly changed as the tops of neighboring trees slipped below the visual horizon and the climber moved into a vast airy space where the only nearby object was the rope. This was a beautiful place from which one could observe unusual organisms in the lower and higher zones of the forest but, unfortunately, there were very few who were able to appreciate this opportunity. Empty space seemed to gnaw at psyches and the more timid were driven to a state of near panic. Rare was the individual who was not in the grip of fear. It was often necessary to repeatedly assure the climbers that once the crown of the monkey pot tree was reached their fear would subside. This claim was always received with much skepticism; our intellect incorrectly concludes that going higher could only make matters worse. Yet those who persisted discovered that, contrary to their deeply believed expectations, the crown environment did bring comfort.

Perhaps on the surface this does not sound noteworthy. Since limbs support weight, they are quite naturally perceived as places of safety. However, most branches en route to the platform were too small to be of solace. Another reason for feeling secure in leaves could be that the ground becomes hidden and its distance, which would normally warn us of danger through reflex, cannot be accurately judged. Even from the platform the ground was always visible because limbs along the route were trimmed to allow unobstructed passage; the ground could also be seen through narrow openings in underlying vegetation. After considerable thought, the only satisfactory explanation was that leaves and small branches, despite their lack of strength, stimulate a comfort reflex. It was as if the presence of many things near eye level in the visual field soothed frazzled nerves.

Finding comfort in a high envelope of leaves that would do nothing to increase a person's security, and becoming petrified in a lower, less dangerous, but exposed position is a paradox of human behavior. The paradox fades when it is viewed from an evolutionary perspective. Our small-bodied ancestors spent tens of millions of years evolving in tropical forest treetops where fear was a normal response in exposed situations, such as climbing isolated trunks or vines where there were no nearby plants to act as safety nets. Great comfort would likely have been felt when clambering among dense mats of small limbs and vines; for small primates, these would have been essential elements of safety.

Observations from the canopy give a new and more logical understanding of the fear we feel near the brink of a cliff. The traditional explanation claims that seeing the depth of a chasm is what gives rise to fear. This is only partially true. Rope climbing has shown that the greatest fear of height is not released by depth perception, but results from what may be a deep-seated primate reflex to an absence of "safety nets." It is this absence of "safety nets" that is most frightening about peering over a precipice. What is most interesting about these new findings is that "safety nets" need not reduce the risk of a fall to release a feeling of comfort.

My supposition that we possess a fear-comfort reflex toward

heights explains why many people are physically disturbed by large windows in tall buildings and cannot bring themselves to venture close to the visual brink even though they are fully cognizant that there is no danger. These same individuals might find comfort in a flimsy curtain simply because it fills a substantial amount of visual space. Airplane manufacturers wisely cater to these primitive instincts when designing aircraft. Small windows mimic a comfortable canopy environment where the ground is visible only through openings in leaves.

I became quite vigilant near the platform because the area often had animals new to me. One day, two least pygmy owls sat at the edge of the roof daintily preening each other. The thought of this still irks me since all my cameras were at the station. When I returned with my equipment the owls were on a distant branch and no longer together. That taught me that I should always carry a camera, a habit that paid off within a few days when a rare hawk, called the tiny hawk, landed on a nearby limb. Little is known about this raptor's behavior except for some isolated reports. The most interesting are those of Gary Stiles, an ornithologist who has seen a tiny hawk fly through the forest undergrowth at high speed to snatch a hummingbird from its perch. The hawk must have had knowledge of where the hummingbird rested as well as astonishing maneuverability since its prey was obscured by a maze of vegetation.

The most conspicuous aspect of the monkey pot's crown were the epiphytes coating its limbs. This botanical wealth included five species of bromeliads, which ranged from a palm-sized plant up to a giant six feet in diameter; there were two species of cactus, several anthuriums, many orchids, two types of philodendron, and a plant called cochliostemmae, which closely resembled a bromeliad. In all, nearly fifty species of flowering plants grew on the branches surrounding the platform, and there is little doubt that if all areas were scrutinized for rare species, that number could double.

It was interesting that the monkey pot's limbs were dense with epiphytic growth while the *Hymenolobium*'s branches were nearly bare. Two features of monkey pot bark make it an ideal growth site: its bark is not rapidly shed and it is deeply grooved, which helps to hold water in the treetop. The traditional explanation that sloughing bark helps trees rid themselves of unwanted plants would appear to account for the *Hymenolobium*'s lack of epiphytes, except for a couple of disturbing observations. Some *Hymenolobium* trees had one or two limbs that were smothered with plants, but these limbs were underneath another canopy tree that produced a continuous rain of epiphyte seeds and perhaps more mature plants; and inexplicably the greatest loads of epiphytes were on another emergent tree species, *Ceiba pentandra*. This tree sheds its bark rapidly, so it appears that sloughing is not the omnipotent cleansing agent it claimed to be.

The platform had no railing so I immediately connected to a safety line, then disconnected from the climbing rope. The air was laden with a pineapple scent from the overripe and sweet-tasting fruit of numerous long-leaved *Sphaeradenia* that dangled from many limbs. I unfolded the cot, unpacked the camera gear, and sat with my feet dangling over the edge. Through field glasses I watched bees and other pollinators as they visited flowering canopy trees, including almendros. A white-necked puffbird dove from a high perch, struck the leaves of the monkey pot, and flew away with a wriggling anole lizard. Black-crested coquettes and other species of hummingbirds drew nectar from sweet-smelling flowers of a large, bushy epiphyte called *Souroubea*, and white-crowned parrots snipped seeds and fruit from a *Dendropanax* tree. At times I saw a resident broad-billed motmot eating insects in the basement.

Over the weeks I watched animals, collected and sampled treetop nuts and fruit, inhaled the scents of exotic flowers, and quenched my thirst with water from the platform's roof. The platform was an idyllic retreat but it was a step backward in the attainment of my major goal: devising ways to move safely through treetops.

People have been building platforms to observe jungle life for at least a century, and inevitably a feeling of imprisonment takes hold. Marston Bates experienced this long ago as he recounts in his book *The Forest and the Sea:*

> In my forest I was always confined to the trunks of the trees [on platforms], I had no way of getting out into "interarboreal space"—I could be a poor sort of monkey, but I had no way of being a bird. In the sea I am one with the fish; I can float or dive or pause suspended in their midst; I must live in a different way, my dreams of floating through the forest, with the birds.

To be like a bird was a tantalizing dream. More and more I wanted to join the butterflies that circled the new red leaves of a *Cespedezia* thirty yards distant, or follow a group of howlers on one of their daily treks through the treetops. To the right of the *Cespedezia* was a seventy-foot-tall *Cecropia*. The *Cecropia* might yield a possible solution to the ant/bare limb problem, but it was off limits to climbers. Not only were its limbs weak, but even the smallest disturbance caused thousands of ants to swarm from hollows within its trunk and limbs. Inevitably a climber would be inundated with a wave of biting ants. Behind the *Cecropia*, a philodendron capped a snag at the forest roof. Yet who would dare climb the tall, rotten trunk to explore the philodendron's story?

These subjects and numerous others remained out of reach since they were located on trees whose limbs would break under my weight. A rough guess would place half of all canopy trees in this category. Yet on their limbs much of the jungle's food was produced, and the activities of birds, monkeys, sloths, insects, and snakes were often centered around them. No methods existed for studying this zone.

A troop of white-faced monkeys headed toward me from the northwest. A ruckus had broken out and angry screams echoed through the forest. Presently the troop turned away and quieted down. Then I noticed frantic rustling in several crowns, a ripple through the canopy. A lone male was speeding in my direction. In compliance with monkey tradition, he had been either ostracized or not admitted to the group. Normally these monkeys are quick to detect human presence, but this individual was totally oblivious to being watched. In primate societies, living in groups is paramount; numerous eyes are far better than a single pair for spotting danger.

This was not always the case. Early primates were nocturnal shrewlike animals that lived in small bushes where they hunted for seeds. On the ground, they sniffed through leaf litter looking for small animals. Their eyes were at the sides of their heads, giving them a wide field of view, much like rats, and they did not need to depend on others to warn them of approaching danger. They lived rather solitary lives.

Living in the canopy began to change these early primates in an unusual way. Over many millions of years, their eyes moved to the front of their heads, giving them binocular vision. It is often claimed that judging distances between limbs for dangerous leaps was the selective force behind the evolution of binocular vision. Squirrels are one of the most successful canopy animals, yet they have lateral-facing eyes. It must therefore be concluded that binocular vision evolved for another reason.

Forward-facing eyes and binocular vision are needed for hunting. Cats, for example, have binocular vision for catching small prey such as mice and birds, while small prey, including squirrels, have lateral-facing eyes to provide maximum security against predators. To aid early primates that hunted arboreal insects, evolution brought their eyes forward and shrank their primitive 360-degree field of view; each incremental reduction in the field of view was conversely accompanied by an incremental growth in the risk of not seeing predators. To compensate for the loss of security, living a solitary existence gave way to foraging in troops, which permitted the full development of forward-facing eyes along with the development of primate social orders that would lead to human societies.

I watched the monkey as he dared to climb a section of a *Laetia* trunk. Once there he spent about an hour running on high limbs, apparently finding the tree's fruit quite savory. When he finally finished dining, he clambered to the lowest limb of the high crown and hesitated, seeming to realize the route down was not going to be the same simple task as ascending.

The risk was too great for a jump, so he hugged the trunk with arms and legs and went down headfirst in a cascade of short little falls that looked quite strenuous. At that moment my heart went out to him. How many times had I made difficult climbs to find that the path down was nearly impossible? The canopy extracts a high fee from monkeys and arboreal apes; many of the long bones of museum skeletons show healed breaks.

Noon brings with it an unusual quiet and it seems all life takes a few hours' rest. Finding the custom agreeable, I lounged on the platform waiting for animals to continue the day's activities.

The platform had a transparent plastic roof held up by four wood posts and a bamboo frame. This was sometimes covered by a red nylon tarp to keep out the midday heat. Animals overhead could be watched through the plastic, and its domed shape collected groups of insects much more effectively than any windowpane. They remained until inadvertently falling to the floor and escaping out the open sides of the platform. Moths and katydids were the largest; black flies, small *Trigona*, and sweat bees were the most numerous. The latter were a major annoyance. Insect sprays more or less repelled the black flies, but only a head net would thwart the sweat bees. Fortunately these were not a constant aggravation.

The assortment of incarcerated insects was a reliable source of intrigue since salticids, or jumping spiders, knew of the cache. I spent many siesta hours watching these corralled insects being stalked by the spiders. Although salticids always take care to lay down an invisible thread of silk as a safety line, they never spin webs. Instead the animals search limbs and litter for living food that can sometimes be ten times their weight. Sharp, long-distance vision aids the hunt, but unlike humans, a salticid cannot move its eyes or head without moving its body. Nature has overcome this restriction with a unique internal eye construction. When peering into a salticid's unmoving, saucer-shaped eyes, one can see them flash and pulse; they are not the usual cold, prismatic structures of insects. The motion comes from light reflecting off the back of the eye where muscles shift the retina across the image plane.

Overhead a salticid stood motionless as its retinas scanned the roof bottom. It walked ahead several inches, froze, and searched again. This procedure continued with mechanical precision until a victim was located. The spider then adjusted its body and leapt with perfect aim. In a few hundredths of a second the back of a katydid's neck was securely clenched between deadly fangs. That same instinct—to catch prey by the neck—is widespread in the animal kingdom and watching a salticid in action leaves one with the distinct impression of an insect-world feline.

Through the light-distorting plastic roof I saw a dark silhouette from a large seed pod suspended directly over my head. Monkey pot trees bear pods that weigh up to seven pounds and are the size of bowling balls. One of these pods once collapsed my roof while I was away and this pod also seemed ready to cause trouble. I got up, assembled twenty feet of collecting pole, and carefully brought the pod to the platform.

The pod's surface was marred by scratches and tooth marks of a very small mammal, perhaps a mouse that had tried to chew its way to the cluster of twenty to thirty nuts. Each nut hangs from a fleshy material that is very nutritious and together they are one of the most nutritive foods in the area. The pod's thick, woodlike tissue accounts for most of its weight and is essential for keeping the natural vault secure against mammals that would not disperse the seeds.

Monkeys, squirrels, and kinkajous will eat sapucaia nuts, but they are designed to be dispersed by fruit bats, which come at night to take seeds after the pod's lid falls free. They carry the seed to a more favorable location, far away from the base of the tree where rodents, deer, rabbits, and other seed eaters spend time feeding. Since bat teeth are too weak to gnaw through the nut's shell, they eat only the fleshy connector, then drop the nut.

The floor at the south end of the platform and two adjacent sides had three-inch-high walls, which kept film canisters and other materials from rolling or being kicked over the edge. Leaves, flowers, twigs, and moisture collected against the walls and in a short time became the domicile of scorpions, centipedes, and ants. I scraped the litter into a pile and uncovered a large spider that measured four inches across, including its legs. A sobering aspect of studying tropical spiders is that little is known about their toxicity. Facts are gathered from medical records after someone has been bitten. I pushed the litter over the threshold, evicting the spider and other inhabitants, but the spider escaped with a long leap. It landed on a limb and crawled in among the epiphytes.

A *Paraponera* trail crossed under the floorboards along the same limb. Only one sting was necessary to convince me of the importance of avoiding these animals. It caused a deep, sharp, burning pain that persisted for several hours. *Paraponera* would stray from their trail to take dead insects from the floor. Although I appreciated the service, I still flicked them off the platform because of my bare feet. Thinking back on this, I regret not having placed an identifying mark on each individual to determine the number of circuits they made to the treetop in a day.

After lunch I put on my boots for a walk to the "crow's nest." One of several limbs on the right side of the platform rose at about a 30-degree angle to the crown's outer surface. Here, smaller branches made a natural observation post for viewing treetops. I stepped onto the limb and steadied myself with a rope strung from the platform to the crow's nest.

Wet moss covered the limb, and near the top it rose so steeply I had to crawl the final few feet. This trip would have been much more difficult had the limb been as overgrown with epiphytes as many of the tree's other limbs. The top of the branch's entire length was an open corridor, which seemed quite odd until I noticed several of the tree's limbs had these same paths. I began to realize that these corridors were probably the result of animal activity in the crown. "Arboreal highways" are as natural a feature of the treetops as animal paths are on the ground. These "highways" were probably maintained by regular animal traffic. After arriving at the crow's nest, I found evidence that the paths might be kept open by pruning; a bromeliad had been trimmed of obstructing leaves down to its base.

At that time epiphyte communities were thought to be unaffected by animal activities, but by exploring the canopy I found instances where epiphytes were both enhanced and hindered by animal activities. The lush bloom of vegetation at the hollow tree, for instance, seemed due to a rain of bat guano, yet the optimum growth sites for epiphytes in the monkey pot tree were worn into paths.

The crow's nest overlooked a shallow valley that originated in the vicinity of the monkey pot tree. The canopy's upper surface dipped as it followed the topographical relief, and formed a canyon of leaves at a permanent swamp where trees did not grow. On the ridges of this valley stood two huge almendro trees with a tall *Hymenolobium* between them. The depth of the valley considerably distorted the true height of the *Hymenolobium*.

This *Hymenolobium* was heavy with ripening peas whose thin, green, elongated pods made the crown appear lush with leaves. Several branches were marked with pink and yellow ribbons where I had artificially self- and cross-pollinated flowers to see if the tree could pollinate itself. The results would show whether or not it was essential for pollinators to fly between distantly spaced *Hymenolobiums* to fertilize flowers. Painstaking work went into placing pollen on the stigmatic (female) surfaces of a hundred flowers.

As I watched, two keel-billed toucans landed in the tree and began eating peas. This in itself was not too upsetting, but soon the birds began ripping pods from the branches where I had been working. The situation quickly worsened as the marauders began yanking my marking ribbons from the branches! I screamed, jumping and shaking the branches, breaking some off and throwing them toward the toucans—but to no avail. The birds were probably accustomed to such primate displays and they casually continued to pull at the ribbons, dawdling away their time until almost none were left. There could be no better demonstration of being prisoner in a tree crown.

I had been oblivious to my surroundings, jumping, screaming, and carrying on near the end of a limb 130 feet above the ground. Many primates, including white-faced monkeys and chimpanzees, frighten intruders in a similar fashion. Shaking limbs and tossing objects is a crude form of tool use, although not a very remarkable one; perhaps a fly, if it had hands and the necessary body weight, could put on a comparable display.

Minutes later seven red-lored parrots landed near the pods and began cramming peas into their mouths, sending me into another frenzy. I knew then that the seeds would not fully mature and I had to get to the *Hymenolobium* immediately in order to salvage data. Returning to the platform, I connected to rappelling bars and free-fell to the ground. Rappelling is a method of effortless descent; one's descent rate is easily controlled by squeezing the rope with gloved hands.

I rapidly scaled the *Hymenolobium*, something I normally did anyway because a swarm of stingless bees were housed in a cavity midway up the trunk. They buzzed incessantly around my eyes and ears and once in a while they delivered a sharp bite.

This *Hymenolobium* was disturbingly limber for an emergent tree, and the whole crown swayed with my climbing motion, a remarkable occurrence since the trunk was a meter and a half in diameter at its base. I rested on a smooth limb high above the bees where I wouldn't disturb them. The bark was crawling with un-aggressive ants of the genus *Chrematogaster* and other insects, including a few weevils. There was a small spider that looked and behaved exactly like one of the ants.

Ants are models for a wide range of mimics found in all levels of the forest. The most convincing was a large spider that looked identical to a *Paraponera;* there are few animals that would tussle with that spider. Mimics are thought to gain some degree of protection against being eaten by lizards, small snakes, and birds.

A green parrot snake crawled up the limb on which I was sitting and slithered by without even acknowledging my existence. These snakes frequent the canopy but are rarely seen as their coloration closely matches that of the vegetation. This serves a dual purpose: a parrot snake can sneak up on large insects and lizards, which are part of its diet, and at the same time be nearly invisible to birds, which are its major predators.

The most spectacular mimic in the forest is *Hemeroplanes triptolemus,* a sphingid butterfly modeled after the parrot snake. The larvae of this species are colored a cryptic green—that resembles twigs until they are disturbed. In one motion the thorax swells—with air and the head end swings free, suddenly becoming the yellow and black head of a parrot snake. This is an effective surprise, of a type known as Batesian mimicry, that would shock even the most resolute predator. As if that weren't enough, the last instar of the caterpillar is another Batesian mimic of the arboreal eyelash viper, *Bothrops schlegelii,* the species I nearly leaned on at the hollow tree. One can only grope to understand the complex processes that brought about this fine-tuned, multiple-mimicry complex.

At the top of the tree I found the remains of my mauled study. Although most of the flags had been removed, all except one of the most important markers remained. These were thin aluminum tags with essential data scratched into their surface. They were designed to weather any storm, but I hadn't considered the powerful bills of toucans.

I was even able to recover data from the branch with the missing tag because tiny aluminum twist ties marked the self-pollinated flowers. Surprisingly, over 80 percent of the self-pollinated flowers were developing pods, within which the clearly visible silhouettes of kidney-shaped peas could be seen. In actuality, little damage had been done to the study.

One group of scientists might suggest that over evolutionary time this tree probably encountered difficulty in having its pollen carried between widely spaced individuals. Self-pollination overcame that obstacle to reproduction. But there is another possibility.

While tallying the results of my experiment, I heard a flock of red-lored parrots approaching the *Hymenolobium*. They inspected the tree as they flew by in formation, flashing elegant scarlet and green plumage. Swooping in a graceful circle, they returned and alighted in disarray. Immediately the birds began jockeying for position. One parrot hopped next to another and both screeched in warning; the submissive animal retreated to a different branch with a plume of pods. In a few minutes they settled down to the business of stripping the tree of its seeds. Between toucans and parrots the pods would be 98 percent destroyed in about two weeks.

This seemed an impossible level of destruction for the tree, but then some seed survival is better than none. It occurred to me that if only outcrossed fruits developed, the tree's overall seed crop would have been perhaps less than one-tenth its present size. *All* seeds from such a small seed crop might have been destroyed by the birds. Perhaps self-pollination was necessary; by producing many more peas than the birds could eat, the survival of a few outcrossed seeds would be ensured.

Some trees may need to produce only a few vital seeds each season to remain in the ecosystem. (The monkey pot, for example, develops about eight hundred seeds per season, a figure that may be comparable to the outcrossed seeds of *Hymenolobium*.) Since outcrossed seeds tend to be more viable than those from self-crosses, even a few outcrossed seeds per season could amount to significant numbers of offspring over the life of the tree.

This brings us to what may be a folly of some tropical research: studying what happens to seeds once they arrive at the ground in order to gain knowledge about how a certain tree species remains a component of the forest. Many trees produce tens of thousands of viable seeds each season and millions over their lifetimes. Seeds and seedlings are extinguished by innumerable factors such as mold, animals, shade, and material falling on them. Studies of how seeds and seedlings die may be interesting, but they are virtually irrelevant to understanding the unique histories of adult trees.

I studied the precision with which these parrots removed seeds from the pods. With its strong beak a bird grabbed a stalk, immediately severing it while holding the plume of pods with one foot. It made a half-moon slit in the pod, using only its beak and tongue, then deftly removed the seed through the slit. I made a very clumsy attempt at removing a pea with one hand.

These were not idle observations; they address the heart of several theories on the evolution of intelligence. It is thought that speech, manual dexterity, and social structure were important features leading to the development of human intelligence. Parrots, unlike other birds, use their feet for grasping objects, but their prowess transcends this remarkable behavior. A parrot bill is the epitome of dexterity; the bird is nearly unique in the bird kingdom in having a kinetic skull. This means that the upper bill is not stationary and can move against the lower bill like a jaw, enabling parrots to be incredibly adept at rotating and moving objects in their beaks. The bill does not act alone; the parrot tongue is equally unusual. Most bird tongues are long, narrow, flimsy affairs, but a parrot tongue looks remarkably like a finger and is a structure of strength. It uses this "finger" like a blind person who has a superior knowledge of how the world feels. The parrot touches and moves a seed to locate the best point of entry, then carefully positions it for cracking. In a real sense parrots have "manual" dexterity.

Parrot social structure is comparable to that of humans in some ways. I discovered this when climbing a 165-foot-tall almendro that held eight or ten nesting Finsch's conure couples. These are medium-sized green parrots with red markings on their heads. The flock screeched at me continually, which in itself was not surprising, but I had a feeling they were giving me unusual attention. The screeching continued and I noticed all the pairs facing me were squawking, moving, or hanging from small vines to attract my attention. The reason for the ruckus was behind me. Two parrots, presumably a male and female, were inspecting a nest hole about eight feet away. I had been duped by the cacophonous flock. While I watched their comical antics, the pair used the smoke screen to check up on their young.

Parrots have dexterity, a complex social structure, and perhaps rudimentary speech. One of the unanswered questions of biology is the purpose of their remarkable ability to mimic human language. Some are known to repeat hundreds of words. There is evidence that parrots can use certain words in their appropriate context, suggesting an understanding of their meaning. Gary Stiles had a pet parrot at his house in San José, Costa Rica, that often said good-bye when someone left the house and hello when someone came in. The parrot was not trained to do this with food reward, nor did she need verbal prompting.

Parrots and humans are both products of the canopy environment as are coatis, an animal that is considered to be one of the most intelligent on earth. The canopy, it seems, has been a potent factory for producing forms of life that have reached a pinnacle in mental development.

I watched the gluttonous red-lores stuffing themselves with peas. They seemed so delighted with the meal that I picked a pod for a taste test, which frightened the flock into the sky. The peas were delicious, but as far as I know they are unknown as a food for humans.

While I was munching peas and enjoying the pristine canopy world, a white, downy feather floated gently by me and headed straight for the monkey pot tree. It crossed the span of weak trees on its way toward the platform. By retracing the course of the drifting feather through the maze of *Hymenolobium* branches, I found I was not alone. A large white bird was quietly preening. It was a rare bird of the forest roof and it had returned to the *Hymenolobium* after a long absence.

Weeks earlier the strange bird had spent its days roosting in the *Hymenolobium*. I had been on my platform with an OTS student making general observations when the bird was spotted eighty yards away. At first it looked like a stump of one of the tree's white, lichen-encrusted limbs, but I perceived a barely detectable movement. I climbed that *Hymenolobium* expecting to find an immature hawk, but this bird seemed like a strange cross between an owl and a hawk. It was nothing like what I had seen before. I asked Buck Sanford, the station manager at the time, to come to the tree and offer his opinion of the bird. He, too, was baffled. Later, Buck talked with Gary Stiles, and upon hearing its description, Gary decided that the bird must be a great potoo.

This was a very exciting discovery because there were no positive records of the great potoo occurring in Costa Rica, even though numerous bird-watchers had been in residence at La Selva and had made a fairly thorough record of birds found there. I took several photographs, the first to be taken of the bird in its natural habitat.

Following the discovery, I was awakened several times one

night on my platform by a "WAA WAA WAA" when the great potoo arrived at or flew away from its roost. This tied a loose end from my first trip to La Selva in 1974. The bird that had haunted my walk on the trail to the almendro was not an owl, but none other than the great potoo.

There are a few reasons why the great potoo had gone undetected by the legions of bird-watchers who combed through La Selva's forests. On certain nights in June and July it was the loudest bird at La Selva, but the call was usually mistaken for that of an owl. In the daytime the bird's cryptic coloration made it nearly impossible to see. Another problem was the description of its call. I found only ambiguous scientific literature; every author seemed to have given the bird a different voice.

Long observation showed that La Selva's great potoos had two frequently used calls. The "WAA" call, which the bird made only while flying, and a very strange sound made only when the bird was sitting. I can nearly reproduce this by drawing air into my lungs while roaring a long, drawn-out "oooorrrr" with deep resonance.

Knowing the great potoo's behavior and vocalizations could make it possible to track birds to their roosts. Its huge mouth hinges behind the ears and seems capable, as has been suggested, of capturing flying bats. Scats found below roosts would answer this question.

Coincidence and observation can carry a naturalist into a tangle of forest mysteries. One find leads to another in a near endless chain of interrelationships. My reason for climbing the *Hymenolobium* was to find the bird, but while there I noticed that the tree would soon be blooming, which provided an excellent opportunity to do controlled pollinations. That led to discovering that the tree was self-pollinating and on and on.

It is this interdependence of life that is so attractive to the biologist. Even distasteful incidents have their lessons. Take feces as an example. Ken Miyata and Adrian Forsyth, in their book *Tropical Nature*, devote four pages to what happens after one eliminates in the forest. A cleanup crew quickly arrives that consists of no less than forty species of insects, most of which are scarab beetles and flies.

I remember witnessing portions of a similar scene that included a practically unbearable degree of jungle savagery. On a small leaf next to some scats I saw a whitish object waving sinuously with the motion of an Indian snake charmer. It was the abdomen tip of an inch-long staphylinid beetle. The beetle was decapitating and consuming a stilt-legged fly, a gruesome sight in itself, but not too disturbing since everything must eat. Then a movement came from the beetle's posterior. Entranced by the motion, another stilt-legged fly was lifting its front right leg to touch the swaying white tip. The incomprehensible deception of this deadly drama gave my sense of fairness a jolt. But the jungle isn't fair, it simply works.

All species are expressions of the jungle's history and each a gear in that dynamic factory of evolution. A parrot in a cage, philodendrons on a deck, or an anthurium in a planter by the window can be no more than curiosities; like the cells cultured from an animal, the meaning and significance of their existence has been lost. The organisms by themselves are impotent forces—none good, none bad—just pieces of the larger entity we call "the jungle."

How little we appreciate canopy life. I recently saw a documentary on the Amazon, and the "explorers," actually a film crew, had severed a vine to show that a fresh drink of water could be obtained from the stalk. We were not shown that above, hidden in the canopy, a beautiful plant withered and died. One vine, I hope, satisfied the thirst of many. Everywhere that visitors and biologists wander in forest basements, life veins of philodendrons and other important lianas and vines are severed because they are inconvenient to step around. We are a species that thrives on destruction; only when something is nearly destroyed do we stand up to protest.

It was near evening when I reclined on the cot back at the platform and ate dinner, with a half-dozen *Hymenolobium* peas for dessert. There were other foods in La Selva's forest that could have supplemented my diet: *Brosimum lactescens*, a canopy tree, has potable milky sap and edible fruit. The nut may also be edible, as Mayans used a meal made from a related species for bread. The silk-cotton, or kapok, tree, *Ceiba pentandra*, is a common emergent whose seeds have a multiplicity of uses. The oil is used in cooking, as a lubricant, as fuel for lamps, and in paint-making, while the seeds are ground into a meal and can be roasted or prepared as soup. In addition, the waterproof kapok fibers are used to make thread, stuffing for cushions, and life preservers. It is also a favorite tree for dugout canoes and rafts. The Guyana chestnut, *Pachira aquatica*, a canopy tree, has a nut whose oil smells somewhat like licorice and is tasty when roasted or fried. The pejibaye, *Bactris gasipaes*, a palm about sixty feet tall, produces a tasty fruit that is widely cultivated in Costa Rica. Edible leaves can be found on some tree species in the genera *Erythrina*, *Cassia*, *Bauhinia*, *Pterocarpus*, and *Pithecellobium*. All bromeliad fruit are edible, as are the pineapple-like fruit of *Sphaeradenia*. This is only a partial list of plants known to be edible. However, eating any wild tropical plant should be approached with skepticism. Not only are there difficulties with identification, but even species known to be edible in one locality may be poisonous in another. The *Hymenolobium* and its peas show that finding unknown foods could be an interesting area of exploration for those with the expertise.

There are also abundant amounts of animal protein to be found in the canopy. Insects, birds, monkeys, and rodents are important foods for many aboriginal tribes and these are not as unsavory as one might think. What a person likes and is willing to eat is largely the result of what he has been raised on. We are especially repulsed, for example, by the thought of eating insects and are sometimes condescending toward cultures that do, thinking of them as destitute and primitive. On the other hand, we regularly eat and relish species of crab, lobster, and crayfish that are little different from insects.

Sundown brought with it a change of music. The chatter of roosting birds and other animals subsided—almost in unison, as if there had been a curtain call for another act. The high, rasping twitter of several katydid species were the first night sounds, and soon afterward large frogs in a distant swamp joined in with deep doglike barks. The outcry of multitudinous crepuscular creatures quickly followed.

Basement shadows coalesced into an impenetrable darkness that became alive with twinkling green specks of light—living stars—the beacons of firefly-like click beetles. I lit a candle and the wandering solitary specks began moving toward me from every direction. The platform was engulfed by a growing, swirling cloud of cool biological fire. The beetles landed on close limbs, making the

Using web rope to catch insects.

Cespedezia petal with female *Lyssomanes* spider.

Head of a large weevil.

The spreading crown of a giant pea tree, *Hymenolobium pulcherimum*.

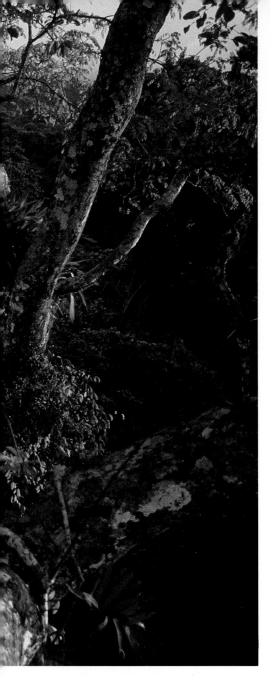

Philodendron flower on pea tree with hemipterans.

Beetles and wasp inside the philodendron's secret scarlet chamber.

Parrot snake and . . .

Canopy orchid.

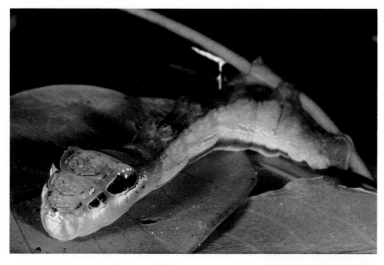

. . . its remarkable caterpillar mimic.

Keel-billed toucan.

Katydid.

treetop look like a Christmas display, and colorful moths darted at the flame. After a while I pinched the candle to extinguish the trance and free the lightning beetles and moths to go about their business.

An extra-fine mesh net was draped from the roof around the platform to prevent pests from getting in. (Tiny biting flies are common in the rain forest and many other places.) I lay down to listen and watch for activity, expecting to see the moonlit silhouettes of large bats arriving to take seeds from a monkey pot whose lid had fallen open in the late afternoon, but none came.

A half hour or perhaps several hours may have passed while I waited for animals; there is something disorienting about the dark that makes judging time extremely hard. I became tired and removed my safety line to be comfortable through the night.

Why can the mind become so very alert and active just before sleep? My eyes were closed but I "saw" the trees and platform as if it were daytime. Suddenly one end of the cot collapsed and I slid off it like a corpse being buried at sea—belly up and head down. I crashed through leaves and branches and became embedded in the ground like one of the tree's seed pods. These were not thoughts that would usher me into a peaceful rest and I felt on the floor for the safety line and tied myself to it.

In the middle of the night a shrill scream startled me from sleep. I searched the crown with my flashlight and found kinkajous feeding on *Clusia* fruit thirty feet above. The animals descended to escape from the light, hand-over-hand and foot-over-foot along a thin vine until they were lost in the shadows of lower canopy trees.

Later a low rumbling awoke me and in my groggy state I imagined the sound to be Arenal, a distant active volcano, spitting ash and lava from deep within the earth. Then I thought it might be the sounds of war, as the Sandinistas were battling for control of Nicaragua, but because Nicaragua was about sixty miles away, any skirmishes would have been inaudible. Since Costa Rica has a politically stable democracy, war was something I didn't have to worry about. Ensuing volleys were louder and accompanied by flashing sky, which washed away my sleepy conjectures; a storm was rapidly advancing.

I got up and untied the bow knots that held rolls of transparent plastic next to the roof. These unrolled to the floor, where they were secured. I lay awake listening to the storm and the incessant chittering of festive treetop frogs who seemed to be working themselves into an orgiastic state in anticipation of the imminent moisture. These arboreal amphibians had always escaped my search efforts so I rose determined to catch one. Their call was deceptively difficult to pinpoint, but after a while I spotted one on a limb fairly near the platform. Engrossed by the hunt, I climbed naked onto the branch with insect net in hand. My bare toes gripped the layer of soft epiphytes, greatly improving my balance. I took several rapid steps up the sloping branch and swung the net; the frightened frog leapt away.

Saltation, or jumping, is an excellent mode of locomotion in treetops as it is one of the more reliable ways to bridge the spaces between limbs. It helps canopy frogs escape from arboreal snakes and other predators since a long leap interrupts the scent trail and cannot be followed.

The frog, a beautiful hylid of about two inches in length, had landed on an orchid ablaze with a dozen or more small, reddish-orange blossoms. I caught it in a sweep of the net and took it back to the platform for photographs. Its translucent green was the green of vegetation, the perfect camouflage in a jungle. Holding the animal close to the light, I noticed it was one of the varieties that for an unknown reason has bones colored by an opaque green pigment.

Croaks of another species came from the tips of distant limbs too dangerous to climb. I could only wonder what that species might look like.

While sitting on the cot and listening to the frogs, I thought of a variety of ways to bring them within reach. A network of catwalks, or rope bridges, could be tied throughout the tree crown, but that idea had an unpleasant side effect: a network would be no small intrusion into the aerial domain. These permanent structures would become alternate routes through the canopy for monkeys and other animals. Diverting traffic from natural arboreal highways would profoundly affect the colonization pattern of epiphytic communities. It is important not to intrude into the workings of the natural world.

The storm hit full force, with roaring winds and sheets of rain that whipped against the plastic walls. The forest was deluged by torrents of water as though a reservoir had burst overhead. Rotten and healthy limbs, vines, and epiphytes were being torn loose from nearby trees and I heard them hitting the leaves of successively lower trees until they finally thumped on the ground.

The monkey pot, which was normally stationary, seemed to come alive, moving its limbs sluggishly like a tanker in heavy seas. Through innumerable cracks the water began its invasion of the platform, immediately soaking everything on the floor, including cameras. I scrambled to protect the sensitive equipment with plastic garbage bags when suddenly a bloodcurdling groan overrode the shrieking winds.

It was the sound of wood stressed to its limit—a tearing, snapping trunk. The tree was falling, and in panic I untied my safety line with thoughts of jumping to another crown. The sound grew louder, almost deafening, like a freight train crashing through wood-frame houses. This was followed by a violent jolt; a giant tree had crashed to the earth and splintered into fragments. A flash of lightning froze the forest's new profile. There was now an immense hole directly in front of my platform where a large *Pentaclethra* had stood.

Wet and sweaty, I stared into the relatively quiet darkness, more than thankful that my tree had been spared. Almost as quickly as it had arrived, the wind died down, leaving gentle rains behind to lick the forest's wounds. I lay down exhausted, fighting the cold and damp with an itchy woolen blanket.

At sunrise my thoughts dwelled on the trials of the previous night. I lifted the rain fly and parted the plastic walls to find wisps of morning mist rising from the newly formed gap. Dozens of smaller trees lined the void, vivified with the sun's potent radiation. Life had given way to new life in the turbulent cycle that keeps jungles vital and ever-changing.

Were it not for luck, I, too, could have been part of that dynamic cycle. A jungle storm will do much to erode one's trust in all trees, except for the scattered, healthy, extremely strong emergents such as almendros and monkey pot trees. Yet since weak trees are the sites of much animal activity, it was essential that a method be devised to make them accessible for study.

That morning I arrived at a solution to the problem. There

were two other emergents near the monkey pot and both were almendros. Stringing ropes between the three trees would enable me to slide out along them on a pully and descend into the underlying forest. The idea had no obvious flaws. The limbs of the trees were definitely sturdy, and with extra-strong rope I anticipated no problems with hanging safely above the smaller canopy trees. I decided to try to build the system the following season, beginning in March of 1979. My spirits soared with the idea of this exciting project.

Spinning a
Canopy Web

AFTER CHECKING to be sure I was
carrying all the necessary equip-
ment, I edged out on a ten-inch-thick horizontal limb in front of
the platform, holding on to a half-inch-in-diameter rope for balance. The limb was covered with large plants and loose moss and
I stepped over them carefully to the spot where the limb sagged
under strain.

In front of me was a system of 1,200 feet of white polyester
rope suspended above the canopy; it looked much like a piece of
abstract art. A rope several feet to my left traveled in a long, gentle
arc from the monkey pot tree to one of the almendros a hundred
yards away. There it made a sharp turn over a pulley and spanned
a hundred yards to another emergent tree. At this tree the rope
made a final bend over a pulley and traveled back a hundred yards
to the monkey pot tree, where it was tied off to a limb on the right
side of the platform. From above, the rope formed a huge equilateral
triangle between the domed tops of three towering emergents. A

final, internal segment of the "web," the rope that I was using for balance, stretched from the platform and connected to the perimeter rope between the two almendros.

Earlier I had rotated the perimeter rope over the pulleys in the almendros so that the internal rope was directly above certain canopy subjects in the tops of some weak trees. My plan was to roll along the internal rope on a pulley connected to my harness. I would then drop a climbing rope into the forest and descend to the subjects. This was a zone that had never been entered by a human.

Traversing a horizontally suspended rope using a small pulley was a technique developed by mountain climbers to cross crevasses, a technique with which I had had no ground-level experience to bolster my confidence. And since the rope web was an untested experimental apparatus, I felt rather like a guinea pig.

In an instant I found myself clinging to the limb while the safety line, which was attached to the internal rope, pulled at my back. The thought of consummating my maiden voyage while dangling from the safety line was intolerable and several breathtaking minutes followed while I struggled to become resituated on top of the branch. While I floundered my hard hat came off, fell for several long moments, and made a sharp thump as it hit the ground 110 feet below.

Ever since the summer of 1978, when I first conceived of the possibility of using ropes strung between emergent trees to study the forest, I had been very concerned about safety. My friend John Williams had a penchant for invention, considerable mountaineering and mechanical experience, as well as a degree in engineering, and he helped to refine my safety plans for the web. Over the next few weeks the "look" of my original system did not change very much, but the way the ropes would be connected to the emergent trees and the function of these ropes had been markedly improved.

The greatest danger in using the web was the tremendous force that would result if the ropes were tightened too much; just as exceedingly large objects can be moved with a long enough lever, improper adjustment could break limbs, snap ropes, and theoretically topple trees. John found formulas at UCLA's engineering library that, after modification, gave us rough calculations on how to adjust the system. These had to be tested so I made a scale model of the web.

For days I played with weights and a fisherman's scale only to discover that the formulas did not predict the test results. The reason for this discrepancy was that the web was more complicated than the rather simple formulas. Ultimately we arrived at the figure for which we had been searching. The ropes needed a minimum of fifteen feet of sag for safe climbing. However, that amount of sag could possibly make the web inoperable; it seemed that the rope might dip into the canopy's upper surface where branches would block the traverse.

During the fall of 1978 and the spring of 1979, I studied at UCLA and laid the ground work for the project. In March, John Williams and I traveled to La Selva and began construction. The most difficult operation was positioning the lines over the forest's roof. My eighty-pound-pull crossbow was not powerful enough to send lines between any of the emergent trees, and this led to grueling work sessions that pushed John and me to the limits of endurance. We experienced heat prostration, dizziness, and a reduced ability to think after spending long periods in the tropical sun. In that foggy mental condition climbing was extremely hazardous; even the simplest of procedures, like tying knots, became a test of wits. Masses of rope, multiple safety lines, and harness straps became tangles that defied our dulled logic.

Three weeks later the web was finished, John returned to California, and I was alone at the monkey pot tree preparing to leap into space. I connected a pulley to my harness, hooked it over the internal rope, and locked it in place. Next I checked the safety line from my harness to a carabiner that rode freely on the rope. I crouched and transferred some of my weight to the rope while listening for the sound of breaking wood. The web was secure. I made one last check on my connections. The web ropes were taut and motionless and I felt a growing thrill, like at the beginning of a roller-coaster ride.

The limb snapped up violently as I jumped off, narrowly missing me as I plunged earthward several feet. The web drooped under my weight, causing a wave to speed along the rope in front of me. The wave caught a resting puffbird unaware and hurled it off the line. I shot from the crown of the monkey pot at a rate of about three and a half yards per second. The pulley whirred as it rode over the braided strands, and a thin rooster tail of filaments flew into the air when the aluminum channel rubbed the rope. I wondered how often that could happen before the rope would have to be replaced.

It was an effortless downhill ride but there was too much sag in the web and I was rapidly approaching the top of a canopy tree. Unable to stop, I lifted my feet and braced myself for the collision. Miraculously, I slipped through the resilient green without damage, although shredded leaves fell like confetti from the tree, which was a bit ruffled by my dangling equipment bags. I watched the platform recede and felt a sense of ecstatic joy as I glided past branch tips, where only the lightest of jungle animals could venture, and into the airways of butterflies and birds. After coasting to a stop and enjoying this new perspective, I was gradually overwhelmed by satisfaction both at having opened up a vast biological frontier for exploration and experiencing movement through the aerial jungle that had hitherto been accomplished only by jungle animals.

A creaking groan, reminiscent of a falling tree, came from the rope and reminded me that my "airworthiness" depended on natural wooden girders and if one of them broke I would be helpless. It was hard to know exactly what might happen, but at a minimum I would be pulled about violently and stretched like taffy through a narrow tree crotch. Soon I realized that swaying branches were responsible for the sound as they "played" the web like a giant violin. These were not comforting tunes; each note wore at the rope, urging me to make inspections at frequent intervals.

I spent the rest of the day pulling myself hand-over-hand along the internal rope, admiring my new study site. The right side of the web dipped into a *Pentaclethra* covered with seed pods. A *Paratropes bilunata*, the cockroach that mimics a lycid beetle, was foraging on the pods, and dragonflies were hunting close to the leaves. On another pod, ants tended a colony of membracids. Membracids, like aphids, produce a sweet fluid called honeydew that is attractive to ants, and in return for this reward the ants "herd" membracids, carry them to new locations, and protect them from insect predators. The tendrils of a bignone vine entangled the tree's branches, and on one of the vine's spirals there was another more ornate species of membracid. Membracids are very unique insects in that their pronotum, part of their thorax, is often ramified into a bizarre structure. Some species look as though they are equipped with a state-of-the-art television antenna, while others appear to be thorns on a branch. The full function of these appendages is still unknown, but it is thought that the sharp appendages are not a good meal for birds, the primary predators of membracids.

Passage along the left side of the web was blocked by treetops. I climbed onto the first obstacle, a *Pentaclethra* limb two and a half inches in diameter, and it instantly broke. The same thing happened in the next tree, a *Stryphnodendron*, and again in the beautifully flowering crown of a *Cespedezia macroloba*. This was an apt demonstration of the strength of many canopy tree branches. In comparison, a one-half-inch-in-diameter limb of the emergent monkey pot tree was capable of holding my weight.

While examining *Stryphnodendron* flowers I found a fine example of protective coloration. A tiny stem I had grasped began wiggling furiously; it was a butterfly caterpillar that had coevolved with the tree, perfectly matching its stems.

Cespedezia has the largest leaves of any canopy tree. They bud from branch tips like red feather dusters. New leaves of many plants are red, turning green after several days. These leaves grow to be three feet long, and when their usefulness comes to an end, they are shed. Like huge gliders, they spiral to the basement. Amid new leaves, shoots of yellow flowers emerge that attract a menagerie of visitors. Translucent *Lyssomanes* spiders stalk the canopy floral garden, blending with yellow petals and green leaves. Many insects visit the flowers, including butterflies, beetles, flies, and both large and small bees, but only large bee species pollinate *Cespedezia*. The weight of a larger bee bends the anthers, which lower the bee against the female flower parts, thereby promoting cross-pollination if the bee has been at another tree.

On a subsequent day the internal rope was positioned directly over a seventy-foot-tall *Cecropia*. I rolled to a stop about ten feet above the *Cecropia*'s crown, uncoiled a climbing rope, and lowered the end past limbs and leaves until it was at the ground. I made sure the rope did not touch any part of the tree as the slightest disturbance was likely to alert its residents, the aggressive *Azteca* ants. I attached the rope to the web and, using the ascenders, climbed down.

Only a few ants were evident in the tree until I struck a limb and touched some leaves. Within seconds the limb was swarming with angry ants that had emerged from holes in the branches. Prepared to attack, the battalion eagerly searched for the trespasser. *Cecropia* is one of many tropical plants that harbor ants. Known as myrmecophytes (meaning "ant plant"), these plants have a mutualistic relationship with ants, a relationship so tightly interwoven that without the other, each species could perish.

To get an idea of how some myrmecophytes evolved, consider a very simple relationship. Some arboreal ants are not very particular about where they make a nest; humus trapped in any epiphytic root mass will do. The plant that has inadvertently offered a living place could still reap some benefit because many ants typically eat herbivorous insects and scare away large animals such as monkeys or adventurous botanists. Over time, a close bond could evolve between particular ants and plants if the plants were to provide ready-made nest sites for colonies.

There are many such myrmecophytes in the world's tropics; La Selva has many different species, including both trees and epiphytes. Some orchids and bromeliads harbor ants in inflated hollows at their base, but usually their ants are not particularly hostile. This would seem to contradict the protective function the ants are supposed to provide; however, a mutualism may be structured upon any favorable relationship.

For example, in Southeast Asia there is an epiphytic myrmecophyte (*Dischidia*) that does very well in forests that are especially destitute of nutrients and organisms in general. It houses a relatively nonaggressive breed of ant (*Iridomyrmex myrmecodiae*) in hollow leaves. The ant's function is not to protect the plant but to provide fertilizer. When the ants forage and dine, their activities produce significant amounts of debris such as unpalatable insect parts and the like. This refuse accumulates and fills portions of the plant's cavities. Eventually roots grow into the composting material to absorb valuable nutrients. By storing their wastes inside hollow leaves, the ants have supplied scarce nutrients for the plant. The plant, in turn, is one of the areas most prolific, thereby supplying the ants with plenty of additional housing.

There is a short, swollen-thorn acacia tree in Costa Rica's dry pastures that has a remarkable relationship with ants. They house an exceedingly fierce species of ant (*Pseudomyrmex*) that frantically hunts down trespassers, much like *Cecropia* ants. *Pseudomyrmex* live in hollow thorns and one colony can have as many as 30,000 workers.

Like garden plants in the wild, swollen-thorn acacias would have a difficult time surviving without their protectors. The leaves of these trees lack compounds that are distasteful to many potential herbivores, and without ants swollen-thorn acacias would be quickly defoliated. The ants also act as gardeners by trimming any vines that may be trying to gain a foothold on the tree and by pruning any vegetation on the ground surrounding the trunk. Without the gardeners, nearby foliage would overshadow and eventually kill the acacia. Not only does this reduce competition for light with nearby plants, but it significantly reduces damage caused by fires that occasionally run through the pastures.

In return for these substantial services, the tree provides more than lodging. A rich food supply, known as Beltian bodies, is produced at the tips of thousands of leaflets. These are minute organs packed with fats, vitamins, and the primary protein source for the colony. The leaf stems, or petioles, have organs called extra-floral nectaries; these secrete nectar as thick as molasses and rich in sugar. The nectar is tremendously attractive to the ants. Together, ants and the acacias are able to live in a region that would otherwise be uninhabitable for either species. Swollen thorns, nectaries, Beltian bodies, and the behavior of these ants are a novel solution to the rigors of tropical life.

The *Cecropia* was no less remarkable than the acacia. It, too, formed a tight relationship with its ants and each provided benefits for the other. *Cecropias* have hollow stems and branches that resemble bamboo where *Azteca* ants can nest; they also have special food organs called Müllerian bodies that are much like the acacia's Beltian bodies. *Cecropias* do not have extra-floral nectaries like acacias, so the ants have found a way of taking nectar indirectly from the tree. *Cecropia* ants tend herds of aphids throughout the tree's hollow branches and stems. Aphids process large volumes of plant juices that, for the most part, are excreted in the form of honeydew, a fluid rich in sugars and other components that the ants utilize.

I had gone into the *Cecropia*'s crown to study an aspect of this relationship that had been in debate. In question was whether or not the ants kept epiphytes from accumulating on limbs. Daniel Janzen, a tropical ecologist, had said that ants probably removed lichens and seeds from the limbs as they arrived, and also chased herbivores from the leaves. However, in nearby pastures some biologists observed that many *Cecropias* were being colonized by vines and the trees' leaves were thoroughly riddled with holes; it was wondered if the ants were providing any benefit at all. To study this I tied swatches of epiphytes, peeled from fallen trees and limbs, in the crown of the *Cecropia*. These were of several sizes, ranging from a thin mat of moss only three-eighths of an inch thick to a half-foot-tall bromeliad.

Ants began mobbing the swatches the moment I tied them to the *Cecropia*'s limbs. The most significant activity was around the thin layer of moss. They ripped at the mat, pulling individual plants free, then walked to the limb's edge and dropped their load. After two days the ants had trimmed all the moss from the limbs. Larger epiphytes, however, seemed to be immune to the ants' activities and even after two years the large bromeliad survived on the limb where it had been placed. From this I concluded that Janzen was correct: the ants must remove epiphytes while they are still seeds and seedlings—the material that normally colonizes limbs.

The probable reasons why epiphytes grew on *Cecropia* trees located in pastures seemed to be that in highly disturbed habitats the ants could not keep up with the onslaught of weedy species, or the ants moved in after the weeds already had a foothold. Since herbivores are abundant in pastures, the ants probably became habituated to unremitting attack. Whatever the reason for these differences, the *Cecropia* ants at my study site proved their worth by keeping weak limbs from being encrusted and broken by heavy loads of epiphytes.

The *Cecropia* ants excelled at repelling intruders. After placing the swatches on the tree, I felt a stinging bite on my neck, soon followed by many more. In seconds I was cursing, slapping, and hastily climbing. Ten feet overhead, ants were streaming from a leaf onto the rope, and as I climbed, it literally rained ants. Even after I had corrected the problem an occasional straggler would come out of hiding and find its way to my skin.

The *Cecropia*'s "caretaker" ants lead me to speculate that ants may be the reason why *Hymenolobium* limbs lack epiphytes. *Hymenolobium* individuals have huge colonies of *Chrematogaster* ants which remove pieces of debris that drop on limbs. It is becoming ever more likely that the dearth of epiphytes on many species of emergent trees may be attributed solely to resident ants, and not to sloughing bark or other factors.

I climbed the descent rope, wound it in, and rolled along the web to station myself above the philodendron. It was only a few yards away from where the great potoo had been roosting in a *Hymenolobium* the previous year. But this time I was suspended on the outside of the tree's crown.

I dropped the descent rope and climbed down next to the huge, lobed leaves of the philodendron, which sat on top of a seventy-foot-tall snag. Though relatively common at La Selva, philodendrons generally remain unnoticed in the forest because their natural habitat is a hundred or more feet above the ground. Seeing them as they exist in nature quickly explains a feature horticulturists might find enigmatic: the numerous rope-like structures that emanate from the stems. These pencil-sized aerial roots have become almost useless in domesticated varieties but are a critical adaptation to arboreal life. Aerial roots can be quite numerous and are frequently a hundred or more feet in length. When seen from the basement these roots form tangled drapes that furnish the only clue of a philodendron's existence high in the canopy. Tendrils are vitally important in conducting water to the huge leaves, which transpire heavily in the full tropical sun.

Technically speaking, philodendrons are not epiphytes. They begin their lives on the dark forest floor as small-leaved vines. After reaching a certain size, they metamorphose and new leaves have the lobed shape with which we are familiar. The main stem loses its connection to the ground and over time the plant moves higher and higher, sending down new tendrils when they are needed.

The philodendron in my study site had climbed to the top of the snag and, finding no place else to go, had become a sumptuous bonnet; even dead wooden monuments hold life in the jungle. I touched one of the leaves, feeling its silken surface, and noticed it was speckled with many small nodules, some of which had tiny holes. These were galls, the nurseries for developing insects. I pinched a holeless gall free from the leaf and broke it open. Inside and nearly ready to emerge was an adult parasitic wasp squirming in fluid from the gall's ruptured walls. On another leaf an adult female squeezed from its vegetable-kingdom womb into a reproductive orgy with many newly emerged males. Older females deposited eggs with long ovipositors into tender budding leaves, completing the wasp's life cycle.

Projecting sensually from the leaf bases were several foot-long monstrosities that looked like hollow pitcher plants. These were flowers—one of the largest in the Western Hemisphere—with an unconventional story that is not yet fully understood. The bisexual flower consists of two major parts: a spathe, which forms an upper and lower chamber, and the spadix, an internal column holding the anthers and ovules. The opening of the pink vulval doors to the upper chamber is accompanied by endothermic heat and redolent of must. No other unrelated flowers produce heat and its function remains unknown.

The fragrance attracts nocturnal beetles and scarabs, which land in the spathe's now-open outer chamber. They immediately crawl down through a narrow portal into the half-light of the inner chamber. It is a lurid world; the spathe's inner surface is a delicate scarlet, and the spadix is filled with pink pillows, which are the plant's ovules. The chamber teems with activity: hemipterans suck fluids from tissues of the spathe, staphylinid beetles consume ovules, and parasitic wasps wander over the pillows searching for a place to deposit their brood. These residents are not beneficial and can be detrimental to the flower. It is thought that scarabs are the pollinators as they fit the floral structure and are found in the lower chamber, though what attracts them there is unclear. Scarabs are dusted with pollen when they leave and carry it to the next flower they visit.

During the following weeks and months I used the web-and-rope climbing methods often to study the canopy. I found about twenty-two species of large bees, some of them new to science, flying among the flowers at the canopy's upper surface. These almost never visited the ground and as a result most were thought to be very rare. They were pollinators of a wide range of canopy species, which included almendros, *Hymenolobiums*, and monkey pot trees.

I found a new class of flower that depends on birds' feet for cross-pollination. To date, I have not been able to locate any writings on this subject. The flower structure is so unusual it may well rank as a new chapter for books on pollination ecology. I studied the plant in the spring of 1986 with the help of Manuel Santana, a tropical biologist, and Gary Stiles. The plant is a tenacious vine, *Norantea sessilis* of the family Marcgraviaceae, whose unique ladle-shaped nectaries produce several cubic centimeters of sweet nectar each day in order to attract birds. Flowers are so numerous that when birds arrive to feast in the morning, nectar literally rains from the plant. I have spent ten years working with flowers and never have I seen so much wasted nectar.

For the vine, attracting birds is only one of the problems of pollination. Ideally pollen must then be carried between plants. Most biologists would not think that the smooth scales on birds' feet could effectively carry pollen. *N. sessilis* is very different from most plants in that its pollen is embedded in a thick, transparent glue. The substance sticks to any smooth surface and easily attaches to birds' feet.

Probably the greatest physical problem the plant must overcome is the mechanical abuse its flowers must endure. Not surprisingly, *N. sessilis*'s female flower parts are small flattened "buttons," and unlike most flowers, they can withstand incredible shearing and compressive forces while remaining viable.

In addition to having a reproductive strategy new to science, the natural history of *N. sessilis* is intimately linked to annual events in North America. *Norantea* has attracted many species of North America's migratory birds: tennessee, chestnut-sided, bay-breasted, yellow and prothonotary warblers, and northern (Baltimore) orioles. A rich flock of exotic and colorful tropical birds have also visited the vine. This knowledge about migratory birds has eluded Gary Stiles throughout years of tropical ornithology. Now Gary is more certain than ever that Central American forest canopies are primary habitats for North America's migratory species (although he sees those birds as fully tropical species that fly north.) I cannot help but wonder if a summer will come when North America's beautiful tropical birds will fail to return because their canopy homes have been virtually destroyed.

Through climbing in the trees I have experienced rare beauty, sensations, and impressions—feelings that can be found nowhere else on the planet. The rewards for biologists who study treetops would now seem limitless, but the pursuit of canopy studies is still hindered.

A few years ago the only method of studying or harvesting canopy products was to collect those that fell to the forest floor or to cut trees and collect the disheveled communities that became scattered at the ground. Field biology is primarily the study of life *in situ*, examining organisms as they are found in their natural habitats. Not one existing scientific research station in the world has the means to study treetop life *in situ*, and a search through a technical library would only uncover a variety of antiquated or largely ineffective methods for observing arboreal environments, such as towers, catwalks, and platforms. One would find a more effective method for observation in climbing techniques akin to those used in mountain climbing. I most often use the climbing methods that I devised, but many other, more terrestrial-loving scientists are awaiting an opportunity to study the canopy unencumbered by the fear of deadly risk.

My present objective is to build the first canopy research vehicle that would virtually eliminate risk and at the same time make a large volume of forest accessible from ground level to far above the treetops. This will be done at Rara Avis, a large tract of land in the misty foothills near La Selva. The site is quite isolated since it is at the end of a several-kilometer-long unimproved trail that becomes knee-deep in mud during the rainy season. Isolation, however, has kept the foothills cloaked in virgin jungle and nearly untouched by civilization. The pristine nature of the area is attested to by crystal-clear streams—now a rarity in tropical regions where logging and agriculture give way to heavy erosion.

John Williams and I have designed an exciting radio-controlled chair lift—The Automated Web for Canopy Exploration—that will transform scientists into "arboreal aviators." AWCE will use the high ridges at Rara Avis to support a network of stainless-steel cables above a small valley. Two researchers using hand-held radio controls will be able to soar anywhere over ten acres of forest roof and down into dense layers of vegetation to investigate the jewels of canopy life. The system will make it possible for all scientists to share in the exploration of treetop life by giving them a freedom of movement never before available.

Besides being used directly for research, AWCE would facilitate construction of small observation platforms as well as a treetop laboratory that might be called "tree-lab." This would have integrated living and working quarters for three investigators and would include a rainwater shower, an insect-free environment, comfortable bunks, and a kitchenette. Researchers could embark on the web and remain in the canopy for extended studies. Together, tree-lab and AWCE would be invaluable tools for basic research.

With the help of Montres Rolex, S.A., of Switzerland, the Heinz foundation, and the Institute of Current World Affairs, the project has begun. Though more funding remains to be obtained, I expect that by the time this book is in print, AWCE will be near completion. Because each tropical forest canopy has its own particular biological wealth and rewards, it is important for research stations throughout the world to have their own AWCE.

A New World
Ecology

A CLOUD HANGS over jungle research. The world is in a reckless race to destroy its tropical rain forests. Norman Myers, in *Conversion of Tropical Moist Forests*, reports that by 1990 logging will destroy nearly all lowland rain forest in the Philippines, peninsular Malaysia, Sumatra, Sabah, and Melanesia. Logging and additional factors such as planned agriculture, slash-and-burn agriculture, and cattle ranching will decimate forests by 1990 in many other countries, including Australia, Bangladesh, India, Indonesia, Sulawesi, Kalimantan, Sri Lanka, Thailand, Vietnam, Brazil's Atlantic coast, Central America, Colombian Amazonia, Ecuador, Madagascar, Tanzania, and West Africa. Deforestation in Burma, Papua New Guinea, Peru, and the Cameroons is perhaps less rapid than in the preceding countries, but nevertheless their forests will also be destroyed by the year 2000.

In 1980, Peter Raven, director of the Missouri Botanical Garden, estimated that 250,000 to 300,000 square kilometers, an area about the size of Great Britain, were being cut each year. Ninety percent of the world's growth in population over the next twenty years will occur largely in the above countries, and these mushrooming populations are expected to accelerate deforestation. By the middle of the next century perhaps all forests will be gone, even in the vast Amazon Basin.

The effects of population growth will weigh more heavily in small geographic areas such as Central America and certain tropical islands. The Amazon, because it is so extensive, will probably be the earth's last outpost of large stands of virgin forest and the species they contain. Yet even now a human wave is washing into the Amazon and bringing change. Frequently this change isn't peaceful.

Bruce Handler, of the Associated Press, has reported that war has broken out between settlers and Brazil-nut harvesters. Between January 1983 and August 1984 more than twenty people were killed in battles for control of the land. Brazil-nut harvesters are trying to protect a $40-million-a-year crop and squatters are seeking relief from poverty and urban slums. The harvesters claim their production is down 40 percent in the last five years because squatters steal the nuts and cut down trees for valuable wood. The actual "villain" is often difficult to discern. Some try to protect the settlers and claim that the harvesters cut down their own trees both for valuable timber and to make cattle pasture, despite the fact that they have received cheap government land concessions granted only for nut production. The harvesters then blame the destruction on settlers. From the perspective of saving forest, mankind is the villain: he only wrestles for the blade to see who will be the owner of a pasture. The future of Brazil nuts looks very bleak.

Other "products" we take for granted that will disappear with forests include primates, parrots, horticultural plants, mahoganies, teaks, rosewood, and, more importantly, hundreds of thousands of animal and plant species whose possible use in pest control, pharmacology, and medicine have yet to be explored. Tropical forests are the earth's largest reservoir of genetic material. As we refine our ability to manipulate this material, an enormous storehouse of inestimable utilitarian value will become available to us. Not only are tropical forests rich in undiscovered species, but even small areas of forest have their own exclusive organisms. Yet, with every passing minute forests are shrinking and we are losing species.

Extinction seems inevitable. The geological record has witnessed extinction on a scale that boggles the imagination. Thomas Schopf, in a paper to the Geological Society of America, states that "probably more than 99.99999 percent of all the species that have ever existed on earth are now extinct." It is an accepted biological fact that the vast majority of organisms on earth today will share this fate.

Although the causes of widespread extinctions are irresolute, there are a variety of possible explanations. To name a few: continents and islands shift position and sink or rise from the sea; ice ages cool climates, and droughts turn forests to deserts. Each cycle helps to extinguish some groups while providing opportunities for others to speciate and flourish.

The extinction of dinosaurs has always attracted much interest, and theories that account for their quietus abound. Over the past several years a variety of media have given considerable attention to the asteroid-collision hypothesis. The prospect of the earth being injured by a wayward piece of cosmic rock at the very end of the Cretaceous, a geological period that ended about 60 million years ago, is irresistible to the press, and the idea even rests on firm scientific ground. The first to discover evidence of this disaster was a group headed by Walter Alvarez in 1979. They found a layer of iridium directly above the last marine sediments of the Cretaceous period. Certain plankton in those sediments disappear above the iridium layer and are thus thought to have become extinct at that time. Now, after much scientific scrutiny, it seems likely that the iridium did come from space. These are the facts and yet the essential evidence is still lacking—evidence that correlates the marine iridium/extinct-plankton layers with extinctions on dry land.

Even Walter Alvarez recognized that the fossil record of terrestrial species would either support or destroy the collision hypothesis. In fact the fossil evidence of terrestrial plants, the best record of what occurred on land, forced a major revision of Alvarez's first proposal. He and his coauthors discussed the issue in a later article entitled, "Current status of the impact theory for the terminal Cretaceous extinction" (1982, *Geological Society of America Special Paper*, 190).

In the dust scenario, we suggested that darkness would last a few years. . . . This was based on a report of the Royal Society of London (1888) which came to that conclusion after a study of the duration of colored sunsets after the Krakatoa explosion of 1883, and which was the only relevant information we had available at the time. Hickey (1981) [a tropical plant paleobiologist] strongly objected to the dust scenario. A few years of darkness should have produced drastic extinctions among plants of the tropics, which do not have the capability of remaining dormant for that length of time, and Hickey did not find these extinctions. . . . Milne and Mckay (1981) calculated that a few months of darkness would produce approximately the degree of extinction among oceanic phytoplankton that is observed in the oceanic [fossil] record. . . . Hickey (personal commun., 1981) concluded that a few months of darkness could not be rejected on the basis of survival of tropical plants.

This indecision over the duration of the dust cloud only partially addresses the weaknesses of the collision hypothesis. Another consideration is that it is difficult to imagine, let alone speculate, about how dinosaurs could be the only major terrestrial group affected by the catastrophe. On a medical level this is comparable to saying that cyanide could kill all types of cancer cells but no other tissue. Alvarez and his colleagues were on the right track when they considered how extended darkness might affect plants. One can only wish that they had fully pursued this line of reasoning by including other terrestrial organisms in their postulate.

To diverge momentarily from this discussion I would like to admit that I am a cynic when it comes to believing most new biological "theories." My experience with academia is that senior scientists all the way down to struggling undergraduates are under a great deal of pressure to produce noteworthy research and theories. To be able to foment biological argument for even a short time can help secure a position at a major institution. This is most easily accomplished by avoiding damning evidence, and it matters little if these arguments soon fade.

A more logical, but perhaps less spectacular, explanation for the extinction of marine organisms is that something poisoned them without affecting the terrestrial biota. Much more attention must be given to this possibility. Knowledge about past disturbance of sea water might provide insight into the consequences of current world-wide human pollution of the oceans.

The asteroid theory has perpetuated the popular belief that dinosaurs came to an abrupt end. In so doing, the theory treaded heavily on the toes of paleontologists who were invited to a symposium to discuss the "Geologic Implications of Impacts of Large Asteroids and Comets on the Earth." The paleontologists concluded that no fossil evidence in existence would support a rapid end to the dinosaurs. As stated in a paper delivered by William Clemens: "Terminal Cretaceous extinctions within the terrestrial biota [dinosaurs, land plants, and so forth] appear to have occurred over a geologically short but biologically lengthy period and to be the result of multiple, interrelated changes in physical and biological factors."

These pronouncements should have extinguished the comet theory; instead they were swept aside in the excitement of imagining ecosystems withering under asteroid bombardment.

At the same symposium Norman Newall suggested that the asteroid theory provided more insight into what people preferred to discuss rather than an explanation of the dinosaur dilemma. "The concept of world-wide catastrophe, death, and destruction appeals to the imagination and is firmly rooted in Western traditions [and religion]." But it is not just tradition that makes us interested in cataclysms. Nuclear warfare and an ensuing "nuclear winter" presents us with some very real threats. Perhaps the fear of self-annihilation is a motive force behind the popular success of the theory. This might be inferred from an article written by Natalie Angier in an October issue of *Time* magazine. The story is unbeatable, bone-chilling rhetoric and if it moves countries to start burying their swords, we will all benefit.

> The stupefying force of the impact, estimated at 100 million megatons, would have generated an enormous 3,000 degree F. fireball that would have spread outward at the speed of sound, igniting forest fires from North America to Asia. Several hundred billion tons of plants and animals would have been incinerated, sending great scarves of black smoke to join the impact dust in the stratosphere and circulate around the globe. What is more, because soot does not rain out as easily as dust, the PROTONUCLEAR [my

caps] winter would have lasted much longer than obscuring dust alone. Most plants and large animals that survived the blast, the fire and the lethal clouds of carbon monoxide would have succumbed to the climatic changes. But smaller creatures could have slipped into caves and hibernated until sunlight returned and then emerged to repopulate the earth.

The theory reminds me of monsters from horror films in which no amount of deadly ammunition has any effect. In general, theories about fossil life are much like monsters because once they have been proposed, they resist death. A good example is the hypothesis that helped get us into this mess to begin with: the one claiming that giant reptiles became extinct as a result of mammals eating all their eggs. There is absolutely no supporting evidence for this hypothesis, yet because no better theory exists, the "egg-eating" hypothesis remains in force.

The fact that mammals survived the Cretaceous and then evolved to fill most niches has led to an unjustified belief that mammals were superior to dinosaurs and drove them to extinction. If so, one would have to wonder why mammals "peacefully" existed alongside the dinosaurs for more than one hundred million years before dinosaurs finally became extinct. This is one of the greatest mysteries of biological history. It would appear that mammals could not out-compete dinosaurs and had to wait for an outside event, such as the colliding asteroid, before they could come to dominance. This leads to some interesting biological questions that have not been answered very well. What was the world like when mammals and dinosaurs lived together? What were the ecological needs of both groups? We will never know for certain the answers to these questions.

Theories about fossil records mirror the beliefs and knowledge of the theorists. It is my view that the best and most probable theories about past extinctions will grow from the knowledge we have about living organisms. For example, there are now sound ecological reasons (see "Extinction of Dinosaurs") why mammals did not compete with dinosaurs for survival. Early mammals were the size of rats and mice and subsisted on insects, worms, dead meat, and perhaps buds and seeds. The plant foods of those times were high in fiber and low in energy. Given what we know about mammals today, it would have been impossible for them to evolve into large herbivorous or carnivorous species because the existing plant communities could not support large warm-blooded animals. In contrast, primitive plants readily supported gigantic, less-energy-demanding, cold-blooded dinosaurs. Mammals abided as relatively small insectivores and scavengers while "waiting" for the ecological energy equation to shift in their favor. This happened during the latter part of the Cretaceous with the evolution of fruit-bearing, flowering plants. And this theory is well supported by available fossil evidence.

Still, as reasonable as the above explanation is, it won't convince proponents of the asteroid hypothesis. But remember that a protonuclear winter descended on all the earth's species. There was no food or light, and everywhere it was cold for a long, long time. Any biologist could determine which animals would have survived those conditions. At this point, the collision theory again becomes shoddy. It is so poorly constructed that it collapses from biological ignorance.

Which animals would have survived? This is a problem of energetics. The animals that used up their stores of energy most quickly would have died. Relative to mammals, the dinosaurs had a distinct advantage, as do all reptiles. To begin with, a dinosaur that is the same size as a mammal needs one-sixth the amount of food to survive. Also dinosaurs would have been able to hibernate, like many mammals, as soon as they got cold. There would have been a large number of small- and medium-sized dinosaurs that could have found shelter. One can only conclude that dinosaurs would have been as likely or even more likely to survive a "protonuclear winter" as mammals.

The coup de grace for the collision hypothesis is that it totally fails at predicting what would have happened to birds. Birds are animals that are literally teetering on the brink of death. They forage in the daytime, and every day they need large amounts of food relative to their body size just to survive. They don't hibernate. Within a week after the cosmic blast, birds would have been totally extinct, yet nearly all major groups of birds survived the Cretaceous and rapidly proliferated. The very existence of birds today proves that there could not have been a protonuclear winter within the last 150 million years, which in turn means a cloud of ash and smoke could not have caused widespread and general extinction during this period. A different sort of event must have finished off the dinosaurs.

Even so, the asteroid theory got another jolt of life from a paper published by D. Raup and J. J. Sepkoski, Jr., which claimed statistical evidence showing that all mass extinctions follow a periodicity of twenty-six million years. But complicated statistics should always be held suspect until others can confirm the results. Even if this proves true, it cannot mean that cyclic protonuclear winters caused extinctions.

If one assumes for a moment that all mass extinctions do fall in a twenty-six-million-year cycle, this theory predicts that the next one will take place about fifteen million years from now. This theory blatantly ignores undeniable evidence that the earth is at a crossroads in its biological history. The leading edge of the greatest wave of extinction since the late Cretaceous is upon us. The National Research Council of the American Academy of Sciences has estimated that by the year 2100 about 50 percent of the planet's species will have become extinct. The cause cannot be blamed on weather, colliding planets, solar radiation, glaciers, or any number of other possible explanations. What we have before us is undeniable and positive proof, something not available for any other theory, that organisms, after taking the next "higher" evolutionary step, can (through *competitive* interactions) devastate the planet's ecosystems so quickly that it could "look" like celestial bombardment, or a protonuclear winter.

There is an egotistical belief by many who say that man is somehow different from other organisms and that the period of extinction we are now creating is unprecedented in the history of the earth. The same thing could be said about the "winners" of each mass extinction in the past.

If one looks objectively at what mankind is doing, it becomes apparent that what is now taking place is little different from Philip Regal's ecological explanation for what happened during the Cretaceous. Rather quickly, from a geological point of view, an arboreal primate stepped to the ground and began growing food and domesticating animals with the use of tools. Access to abundant and reliable sources of food allowed for increasing "leisure" time and intellectual achievement in fabrication of tools. Through natural selection, man improved his domestic crops and animals (there is no such thing as artificial selection) and the ecological system rapidly evolved. New intellectual strides and tools increased the range of climates and habitats where humans and associated domestic animals could survive. The relationship between humans, domestic animals, tools, and an ability to utilize ever more complex forms of energy is the most powerful synergism ever to have come out of the evolutionary process. Predictably, this synergistic community is systematically overrunning all available ecosystems, just as the bird-insect-angiosperm synergism extinguished the dinosaurs.

No single species in the past has had an ecological impact as broad as that of *Homo sapiens*. Our cleverness has made us the most numerous of the planet's large beasts. It is estimated that by the year 2000 another two billion people will share the globe and its resources, which are already in short supply. Since overpopulation and a lack of resources can be implicated in most crimes and human suffering, it would seem logical and certainly beneficial for every organization in the world, religious and otherwise, to recognize that the population explosion is the number one threat to our planet, not nuclear weaponry.

It is possible that we could still save tropical forests and ourselves, but we need not blame other less fortunate people for devastating the planet's ecosystems. Each of us is responsible. The present world crisis brings humankind to the end of a long period of self-infatuation. Above all else we are braggarts of our collective mental capacities and idolaters of ourselves. This is especially obvious in an art museum where one can find innumerable paintings of people, filling wall after wall in a monotonous series. Similarly, books on human evolution ring with complacent wisdom about the remarkable climb of *Homo sapiens* from the dark abyss of animal ignorance into the dawn of self-awareness and intelligence. Even our gods are made in our image. The stories are told as if it were somehow miraculous that evolution coughed up such an amazing mental creature. The human brain is no more wondrous than a flower, feather, or any other adaptation.

What if other organisms spent most of their time patting themselves on the back for their particular evolutionary specialization? The elephant could lumber about cooing, "Oh my trunk, my trunk, my trunk, my trunk, my trunk. What a very exceptional and elegant organ! There is no other animal on the planet that has this exalted, miraculous manifestation of evolutionary perfection!" The insects would scream in buzzing and annoying unison, "Brains! Who needs brains? Brains have not helped the large-skulled beasts. We will continue feeding on them, reproducing, dispersing, and hiding, and we will be here long after they are gone. Ours is a perfection sculpted in heaven. We are the chosen multitudes." All sorts of vermin, rats, snakes, butterflies, parasites, birds, clams, fish, snails, centipedes, scorpions, squirrels, beaver, and bears would be squawking, croaking, snorting, bellowing, squealing, crowing, chortling, and filling the air with the most intolerable racket.

Man is an animal, no more or no less. Humans are not to blame for the devastation caused by our evolutionary condition any more than a rat is to blame for the fleas that carry bubonic plague. We are merely animals that have taken both a small and a large evolutionary step, a small step in that we are still 100 percent animal, a condition that we will never be able to escape, and a large step because our minds can imagine a reality unknown to our genes, a world where all forms of life are viewed with compassion.

It seems inevitable, looking back on the angiosperm-energy revolution and the need for powered flight, that it would be only a matter of time before an organism, through knowledge, would discover the secret of "free" energy. Our progenitors did not eat from the Tree of Knowledge, they were borne from trees of knowledge in a jungle's roof; the brain fashioned there has gone on to exploit the next level of environmental fuel. Like the synergism uniting trees to birds, this, too, is an energy revolution molding man to machine. This is not the fault of man, for he is propelled by the basic animal desires to satisfy physical and social needs. The success of our species' search for energy is only now coming to a climax. The result, unless more people come to the aid of forests, will be that only a few decades remain in which you, and your children, will have the opportunity to appreciate and study the most complex and interesting communities of life to ever have blessed the earth.

"Life, even cellular life, may exist out yonder in the dark. But high or low in nature, it will not wear the shape of a man. That shape is the evolutionary product of a strange, long wandering through the attics of the forest roof, and so great are the chances of failure, that nothing precisely and identically human is likely ever to come that way again," wrote Loren Eiseley in *The Immense Journey*.

Twenty million years from now, long after the planet has crawled with billions of the hopelessly starving, long after man has driven nearly all other species to extinction, and beyond when we see to the depths of our despondent spirits and intellect, and past the stage when we judge ourselves incompetent to live and rule by using poisonous and morbid tools of destruction, then and only then will tropical forests again raise their crowns in luxury, to feast in the warm sun. In that canopy there will be arboreal beasts, and I do not doubt that some will descend from the trees to cross our clever course. Perhaps one will stoop to wonder over fossilized remains and discover that another bipedal species had preceded it from the trees. And just maybe it will be a marvelous creature that takes a higher step in the mental plane and treats the planet and its inhabitants in a manner about which we have only talked.

Bibliography

Bates, Marston. *The Forest and the Sea*. New York: Vintage Books, 1960.

Beebe, William. *Tropical Wild Life*. New York: New York Zoological Society, 1917.

Colbert, Edwin H. *The Age of Reptiles*. New York: W. W. Norton & Company, 1965.

Darrah, William C. *Principles of Paleobotany*. New York: The Ronald Press Company, 1960.

Eiseley, Loren. *The Immense Journey*. New York: Vintage Books, 1957.

Forsyth, Adrian, and Ken Miyata. *Tropical Nature*. New York: Charles Scribner's Sons, 1983.

Heilmann, Gerhard. *The Origin of Birds*. New York: Dover Publications, 1972.

Hudson, W. H. *Green Mansions*. New York: Random House, 1944.

Janzen, Daniel H. *Costa Rican Natural History*. Chicago: The University of Chicago Press, 1983.

Menninger, Edwin A. *Edible Nuts of the World*. Stuart, Florida: Horticultural Books, 1977.

Murray-Aaron, Eugene. *The Butterfly Hunters*. New York: Charles Scribner's Sons, 1903.

Page, Jake, and the Editors of Time-Life Books. *Forest*. New York: Time-Life Books, 1983.

Romer, Alfred S. *The Vertebrate Story*. Chicago: The University of Chicago Press, 1959.

Seeley, H. G. *Dragons of the Air*. New York: Dover Publications, 1967.

Twain, Mark. *Life on the Mississippi*. New York: Harper and Brothers, 1896.

BIBLIOGRAPHY

Index

169

About
the Author

Don Perry, a full-time biologist, explorer, writer, and photographer, spends much of his time traveling to satisfy his continuing curiosity about the hidden biological treasures of the earth's jungles and forests. He has been a contributor to several films on wildlife and has been widely published in scientific journals and popular magazines. He is also the author, with S. E. Merschel, of the children's book *Journey into a Hollow Tree*.

Perry, thirty-nine, holds a Ph.D. in biology from UCLA. He lives in Branchport, New York.

It is my hope that tropical forest canopies will be saved and studied for the pleasure and benefit of future generations. With this in mind, I am beginning several long-term canopy research projects. Those who may be interested in helping to fund this work can make fully tax deductible contributions to the University of California Foundation by contacting me at the following address for a contribution form:

Donald Perry
1341 Ocean Avenue, #154
Santa Monica, CA 90401